THE
INSHALLAH
PAPER

To David Lucas,

The Best Night Editor

in Fleet Street.

With Best wishes,

October 21, 2009

Inshallah – if Allah wills (*Concise Oxford Dictionary*)
– this week, next week, sometime, never (common usage)

THE INSHALLAH PAPER

Andrew Trimbee

QUARTET

First published in 2009 by
Quartet Books Limited
A member of the Namara Group
27 Goodge Street, London W1T 2LD

A catalogue record for this book
is available from the British Library

ISBN   978 0 7043 7175 0

Typeset by Antony Gray
Printed and bound in Great Britain by
T J International Ltd, Padstow, Cornwall

FOR CHRISTINE

LEONA, SARAH, JAMES AND RACHEL

ACKNOWLEDGEMENTS

I would like to thank my friends Anwar Abdul-Rahman of the Al Hilal Group for his help with background detail of Bahrain; Abdulla Khan of the Bahrain House of Photography for permission to use his pictures; Jassim Al-Ameer for his hospitality and wisdom; and Margaret Bury for her research and technical expertise, without which both my manuscript and I would have been lost

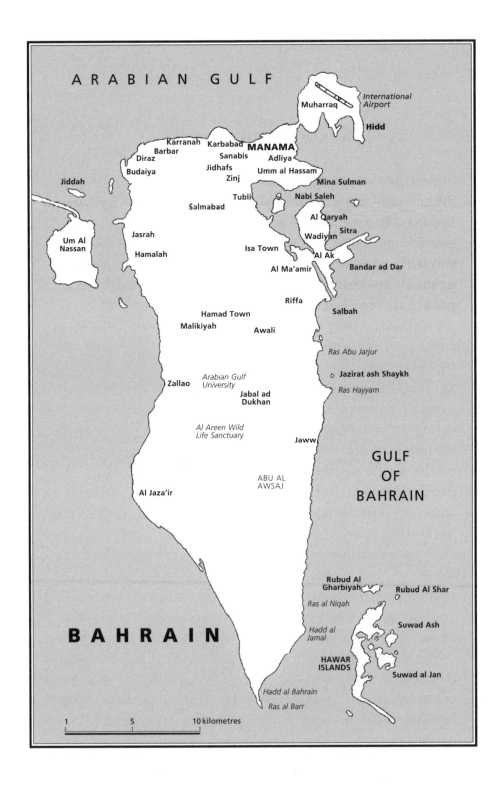

CHAPTER ONE

Through the haze of cigarette smoke a figure wove his way towards me, threading his way past gossiping groups of Arabs, Europeans, Indians and Americans who thronged the terrace. 'I should warn you. The infant mortality rate of newspapers in Bahrain is high.' If this was a greeting, it was also a less than encouraging putdown by the former Fleet Street cartoonist as he thrust a drink into my hand.

I had arrived only that morning as the sun rose on the dusty island sheikhdom of Bahrain, in the Arabian Gulf. Jet-lagged from the ordeal of a nineteen-hour journey from Heathrow, after being left stranded in Beirut, I was still reeling from the strangeness of it all and, it must be said, from no small amount of culture shock.

Now I was having cocktails in a palm-fringed garden as the winter sun went down, surrounded by strangers, not all of whom exuded a great delight at the arrival of this fledgling editor who had left behind a promising career in Britain's world of print to launch a newspaper in a faraway country about which most people knew little.

An inauspicious debut, as the weekly newspapers in the shires would say. But if I felt abashed, I didn't show it. At the age of twenty-eight, I still had that brimming confidence of a young man and an unshakeable belief in my own abilities. That belief was to be sorely tested in the months that lay ahead.

The Middle East Airlines flight from London had passed over the Alps, with the snow-covered peaks brilliant blue-white in winter sunshine. As we crossed Greece, plumes of smoke rose high into the air from remote villages barely visible on the brown parched earth. We arrived late in Beirut, and I then had to endure a seven-hour delay before the connecting aircraft took off on the onward leg down to the Gulf. We were well on our way when the captain announced that we were turning back. Apparently, because of the delays, the flight was so late that the cabin staff had worked beyond their permitted hours and a crew change was mandatory. By this time I was utterly fatigued through lack of sleep and almost despairing of reaching Bahrain. If I was feeling downcast, my neighbour in the seat next to me did little to raise my spirits. He was a Scotsman, travelling to Saudi Arabia to work on the giant compressors that produced ammonia for fertiliser, breaking it down from the well-head gas. He anxiously pointed to the orange light glowing on the underside of the wing, and reflected from the aircraft's flashing belly light. 'Are we on fire?' he hissed. If we were, I was beyond caring.

After such an exhausting flight I was in no mood to appreciate the island's charms as dawn broke over Bahrain. Dust. That was my first impression. A grey dust that seemed to hang over everything, cloaking the palm leaves, the white houses, the uneven roads and the mosques. 'It's not a bad place, you'll get to like it,' said a cheery James Belgrave, the 6ft 5in son of the island's former adviser to the Ruler, whose brainchild this first newspaper was. 'You're not seeing it at its best.' You could say that again. Not for the first time, I wondered if I had just made the biggest mistake of my life.

The ruddy-cheeked Belgrave, whose joviality belied a basic shyness, wove his car in and out, avoiding donkey carts and pedestrians as he negotiated the roads into the capital, Manama, crossing the mile-long causeway from the airport island of Muharraq with the waters of the Gulf, choppy from a brisk breeze, gleaming around us. Minutes later we pulled up outside his imposing house, in a leafy garden suburb where the pink and white blooms of oleander bushes brought a splash of colour to the otherwise drab surroundings.

Belgrave showed me to my bedroom. High in the wall above

the bed was an oblong brown box covered with dials. A sturdy black flex led to an electricity socket. 'That's the air-conditioner,' he explained. 'No need for that in winter.' It was an essential item of equipment that I was to become very familiar with. 'Well, you'll be needing some sleep,' said Belgrave breezily. 'I'll be getting along to the office now, and catch up with you at lunchtime.'

But in truth I was well past the ability to sleep, despite having had none since six the previous morning when the taxi arrived at my home in the north of England to take me to the nearby airport. Zombie-like, I turned down the sheet, laid my heavy sheepskin coat on top of the bed – little use for that here – and climbed in. After an hour, still unable to sleep, I got up and explored the house. Nice, big, comfortably furnished – and deserted. Enid, Belgrave's down-to-earth buxom wife, was still in the Home Counties, preparing to return with their two young daughters. Indus, their servant, well, God knows where he was. I tiptoed around, craning my neck round each corner. An impressive array of bottles, brandy, whisky, gin, crowded a sideboard laden with Georgian silver. A dark brown cigar humidor, its drawers full, I noted, of crumbling Montecristos of varying sizes. In the kitchen, an enormous fridge. I opened the back door and pushed aside the flyscreen. Stacked outside, shoulder high, were pile upon pile of wooden cases stencilled Booths Dry Gin. Each was full – of empty bottles. Hmmm, I thought, I'm going to like staying with the Belgraves. I was to find that you can have too much of a good thing.

Belgrave reappeared for lunch, served by the inscrutable Indus, then we drove into the city centre to meet his office staff, making a detour to show me what few sights there were. The police fort in the centre, massive crenellated thick walls, with the British-trained sentries erect and alert. The dhow quay, where the great teak boats that have plied the waters of the Gulf for hundreds of years berthed with their cargoes of spices, Persian carpets, rice, onions, oranges . . . and air-conditioners, cookers, fridges, fans, gas bottles, a whole host of consumer goods that were bought and sold on both sides of the Gulf. Further out, the crumbling ruins of a Portuguese castle, a reminder of the short-lived rule of one of the world's greatest seafaring races; the deep-water jetty of Mina Sulman, way out past the British naval base of Jufair; a 1,000-year-old burial ground, with the faded white outlines of the skeletons in their shallow graves, dust to dust.

In Belgrave's office, an offshoot of a Mayfair public relations consultancy, the staff introduced themselves, curious about this newcomer who was foolish enough to throw in his lot with what I was to find many believed was a pie in the sky project: Louisa, his striking blonde secretary married to a British Airways engineer; Ahmed Fakhri, his helpful Bahraini second in command; Roger, his able and personable art chief; Bruce, a talented graphic designer who, having lost an eye, wore a piratical black patch.

As I sat there I felt it was time, indeed high time, to broach the subject of where I was to live. I had been assured in London that Belgrave 'would be sure to find somewhere pleasant'. 'Er, about my home, James.'

'Ah yes. We can go and have a look now, if you like. It's in the same building.' A messenger was despatched to get the key. We took the creaking lift back down, and walked along a corridor where the white-painted concrete was already spalling, the re-inforcing bars clearly visible; the building was only a handful of years old but the effects of the corrosive salt-laden Gulf air and second-rate construction were beginning to show.

Belgrave unlocked the door. A view swam in front of me like a mirage. It was beautiful. The waters of the Gulf, now with the sun on them, twinkled; dhows moved slowly across; palm trees fringed the road several storeys below; to the right, the modern building housing the government, with its honeycomb cladding, gleaming white. 'James, it's perfect,' I said. 'Ah yes.' He coughed. 'This was to have been your home, but unfortunately the owner has now decided he wants to keep it for his own use. We'll have to find somewhere else.' For God's sake, I thought peevishly, why bother to show it to me in the first place. The question of my future accommodation was to become an issue that threatened a slow erosion of the goodwill with which I had been overflowing on my arrival. The towering Belgrave, an upper-middle-class Briton, Bahrain-born, was to prove irritatingly Arab in his outlook.

'We'll deal with your accommodation in due course,' he said as he locked the door behind him, cutting me off for ever from that tantalisingly idyllic view. 'You've very welcome to stay with me for a few days, and then I've arranged for you to move in with a friend until you find your feet.

'Tonight, a cocktail party to meet some of the people who help make Bahrain what it is. Tomorrow, we'll see the newspaper's office, tour the printing press, and meet the people you'll be working with.'

CHAPTER TWO

But first we had to meet the Ruler. The next morning we drove the eight miles to Rifa'a, in the middle of the island and seat of the Al-Khalifa, where a handful of houses clustered around a low hill, with a makeshift racecourse – for camels as well as horses, overlooked by a ruined abandoned palace clinging to the edge of a rocky escarpment.

Just off the road was a long light-brown building, with an entrance surrounded by wrought-iron railings and next to its own mosque, with a low white dome. More cars arrived every minute, the drivers jostling for a parking space. Armed Bedu guards swathed in bandoliers of ammunition stood discreetly by. Belgrave and I walked through the gates and through an arched doorway, stepping over Persian carpets as we entered the main majlis, a large rectangular room that seemed almost as big as a football pitch. The seats along the sides were packed with local merchants and petitioners, the bright white of their freshly-laundered robes contrasting with the gold-edged winter cloaks of black and brown. There was a handful of Europeans, and the Ruler's English personal secretary, a popinjay in full morning dress. I wrinkled my nose at the aroma of oud, the sweet smelling incense-like wood burned among glowing charcoal in metal vase-like containers.

We squeezed in, and waited. Suddenly the entire room was on its feet as the doors swung open. A tiny figure resplendent in richly-coloured robes, with a golden headdress and his ample middle encircled with an ornate gold dagger, glided up the centre of the room, followed by his closest retainers. He took his seat at the top of the room. 'Salaam alaikhum.' His voice rang out, strong, authoritative.

14

His Highness Sheikh Isa bin Sulman Al-Khalifa, though barely five feet five inches tall, possessed that rare quality: presence. In that instant, he had the entire attention of that crowded majlis. His voice rang out again. 'Ga'hawa!' The armed guards took up the call. 'Ga'hawa', 'Ga'hawa', 'Ga'hawa', the voices fading as the call was passed on down the hall and then outside. The response came quickly. First faintly. 'Inshallah!' Then stronger and stronger again, as it was relayed. 'Inshallah', 'Inshallah', 'INSHALLAH!'

Suddenly the doors swung open again and a phalanx of six retainers marched in, each carrying a large brass coffee pot in one hand and, in the other, a stack of tiny porcelain cups that clicked and rattled as they strode up the hall. A jet of green-gold liquid arched through the air, splashed into a cup and it was handed to the Ruler. Gradually they moved down the sides of the hall, dispensing the bitter Arabic coffee, flavoured with cardamom seeds, then moved round again for a refill. A third cup was usually refused, with the traditional sign of shaking the cup from side to side, a tiny movement using finger and thumb. Any dregs were unceremoniously tossed aside, to be absorbed by the deep-piled British Axminster carpet that covered the whole of the floor of this inner sanctum.

The head of the local radio station leapt up, crossed the floor and knelt at the side of the Ruler, handing over a list of the world's headlines that morning, to be received impassively, before darting away. Others advanced with scraps of paper, requests for help, a sick child, a brother in trouble, a plea for an airline ticket. All were collected by one of the Ruler's clerks, disappearing into an inner pocket of his robe, later to be emptied out on to a table in one of the offices where urgency, desirability and diplomacy would all come into play in deciding action. The final word lay with the Ruler's Household Treasurer, an inscrutable, sly little vizier who controlled the purse-strings on behalf of his master and a man respected and detested in equal measure by all petitioners. Would help be forthcoming? Inshallah.

The day's formalities now at an end, the Ruler lifted his head. 'Chai.' As before, the call was repeated down the hall, out into the courtyard, round the corner, fading away. Back came the reply, and within minutes in marched the same retainers, this time bearing garish enamel teapots with hooped handles, dispensing hot, sweet tea – two cups – which denoted the close of business. The hall rose to its feet, and as the Ruler moved towards the door, a bearded black-robed servant plucked Belgrave by the sleeve. 'His Highness would like to see you afterwards.' We resumed our seats.

Minutes later we were escorted out of the hall and into a tiny nearby room, the floor covered in fine silk Persian carpets, where Isa was waiting on a settee. He rose to his feet and came towards us.

As Belgrave made the introductions, he turned to me. 'Welcome to Bahrain.'

His English was beautiful, with barely a trace of an accent. He asked where I was staying, when had I arrived – this, I was to find, was always important to an Arab: just how long had you waited before paying those vital formal respects – and where had I come from. 'Bahrain needs an English language newspaper – and we need a proper newspaperman to produce it,' he told me as, tongue-tied, I stumbled over a few words of carefully rehearsed pleasantries. 'We wish you luck. If you have any problems, come to me.' His smile was warm, his courtesy old-style, his manners impeccable. In came the coffee, followed rapidly by the tea. The meeting was over. He shook hands again, the highly perfumed scent he was wearing still clinging to my palms hours later. The doors closed behind us.

'You made a good impression,' said Belgrave, fluent in Arabic but who had spoken in English to the Ruler throughout. Little was I to know just how important this diminutive regal man was to become to me, and how vital his support would be in this forbidding project of launching – and running – this newspaper, the first English language newspaper in the southern Gulf.

The vital business of the introduction complete, we joined the long tailback of cars, from the latest Mercedes, Jaguars and Japanese saloons down to the battered rusting wrecks that one would expect to find in a scrapyard, that crowded the road down into Manama.

'Right, let's see your office,' said Belgrave. We took the lift at Al-Moayyed Towers, the same building that housed his own suite of rooms, and arrived at the fourth floor. The door swung open. I saw streaked uncurtained double windows, a steel table, one office chair, and a telephone on the floor. There was nothing else. A small, neat figure in a dark suit and tie advanced towards us. 'I am Thomas,' he announced, slightly pompously. 'Er, yes, I forgot to tell you,' said Belgrave. 'This is the assistant editor. He was recruited by my staff in India. We thought you'd need some help.'

K. A. Thomas – always known as Thomas, I never did find out what the initials stood for – was a newspaperman from Kerala, the son of a judge. This was his first visit to Bahrain; I wondered if he knew what he was letting himself in for. No equipment, virtually no furniture, no other staff, and the print works still an unknown quantity. Clearly, there was much that had to be done. Was it too late for second thoughts? Yes, it was. I had left behind a key job with one of England's leading provincial morning papers. Going back was not an option. My bridges had been well and truly burnt. Like it or not, I was here to stay.

'Time for a drink?' The voice of Belgrave broke into my thoughts. 'Nice idea James, but first show me where I can buy some furniture.'

Barely an hour later, in the large high-ceilinged showroom of Abdul-Rahman Al-Moayyed, courtly softly-spoken brother of my office's landlord, I had bought more desks, filing cabinets, chairs, bookcases, ledgers, cups, saucers, glasses, a tiny fridge (vital), stationery that ranged from reams of A4 copy paper to envelopes, files and carbon paper, and then added staplers, pencils and erasers, finally ending with drawing pins and paper clips.

As I signed the increasing number of chits, my first purchases drawn on the barely existing bank balance of the *Gulf Mirror*, coolies – the capital's delivery boys, white cloths wound round their heads – were already bustling, assembling the long list of items and bearing them out and upstairs to the office. I turned to Belgrave. 'About that drink.'

CHAPTER THREE

With the furnishing of the office underway, it was time to inspect the press. The Arabian Printing Press was housed in a grubby two-storey building, light brown paint peeling on the double doors, concrete steps, as usual cracked, leading up to the entrance. Rubble, debris and litter lay around outside; in the street, exposed to the winter weather and glare of the summer sun, were four wooden crates bound with steel straps. They contained one brand-new dismantled English Linotype machine, imported at a cost of £10,000. The packing cases were to lie there, unopened, for three years, over the road from a tiny shop and one of the mosques that seemed to surround the print works. Inside, I was met by a waft of that particular aroma known to all journalists, made up of the smell of newsprint and the pungent reek of printing ink.

As the sun filtered through the grimy windows, I could make out figures toiling and heard the clack of type-setting, making up headlines using the time-consuming process of assembling the letters by hand, the tinkle and rattle of a Linotype, the wap-wap-wap of a tired old press which was used, laboriously, to produce galley proofs: the only way they had. The Indian printers, teeth shining white, seemed eager to please, smiling and friendly as they worked the incredibly long hours that they had to do to send money back to their families in Goa. I was introduced to the manager, Mr George, who was dignified but wary of this western journalist. The head of the rival printing firm, Oriental, was also called Mr George. I later found this would lead to considerable confusion. The overseer, Matthew, was chatty, bright and, as issue relentlessly followed issue, seemingly untiring. He proudly pointed out the tiny white-painted room which had been set aside for the *Gulf Mirror* staff, lit with one dangling bulb and with one battered small table, for proof-reading, and one chair, also battered, but with the luxury of a brand-new air-conditioner, added, I found out later, as an afterthought.

Working away at a low glass-topped table was Fikhri, the Egyptian paste-up artist who, when the proofs were corrected and approved, would slice away the borders with a razor blade and, using a ruler and set square, or sometimes relying just on his eye, stick them down on a blank page, marrying text with headline, picture with caption, using tiny segments of Sellotape, then drawing in the column rules with a ballpoint pen before a photographic plate was made. It sounds laborious, and believe me, it was.

Finally, there was the owner, a former bank manager and, of course, a local Bahraini. He would sit upstairs in his cluttered office overlooking a dusty palm tree, filling his pipe with English tobacco, overweight, rascally, and with a quick humour, as he penned his latest waspish leader for his own Arabic newspaper. At night, the windows would glow as the work went on. One evening, returning to the press, I was preceded up the steps by a large rat. I thought it summed the place up.

I reported back to Belgrave, who seemingly occupied a different world far removed from the trials and traumas that were to be mine as the weeks unfolded. 'Well, what's your impression?' he asked. 'Everyone seems to think it can't be done. The public relations people at the local petroleum company say the press just isn't capable of producing an English language newspaper.'

I took a deep breath. 'Yes, it can be done. It won't be easy, but it can be done.' 'Okay, what's the timescale?' It was December 15; it had been decided that publication day would be every Sunday, to include the English soccer results of the previous day; Bahrain is a soccer-mad island. I looked at a calendar and committed myself. 'The first issue will come out on January 3.'

The die was cast, a particularly apt metaphor, I thought, as I walked out for a good stiff drink. Now I needed some staff. First, a secretary. Enter Beryl Parr, wife of a British economics lecturer at a local college. I had found her by using the grapevine of the small expatriate community. Beryl, dark and attractive, with her hair in a fetching ponytail, turned out to be a pocket dynamo who entered into the challenge of setting up a new organisation with an awesome efficiency and enthusiasm. Within two hours of her arrival, a large typewriter stood on her desk, a delivery man had loaded up the mini fridge with soft drinks and she stood, pad poised, as I rattled off the first of scores of letters. We needed a horoscope each week. The Central Press Agency in Fleet Street had supplied the same service when I worked on the *East African Standard* in Nairobi. A deal was struck and the first horoscopes – six weeks' worth –were in the mail within days. I could hardly fill the paper on my own, and I negotiated a cut-price deal to take the Reuters wire service. A recurring nightmare was that I had left the teleprinter on all night, and sometimes I did; I would arrive in the morning to find literally two dozen feet of Reuters news lying in paper coils on the floor. The service was to prove a great help in filling corners: 'Kurds are revolting', 'North Yemen leaders blown up in tent while at peace talks', 'Oapec reviews its pricing strategy'. But the mainstay of the paper was to be local news.

No sooner had the phone been connected up by Cable & Wireless than it rang. It was James, two storeys upstairs. 'A bit of good news. Bapco has agreed to second Jim More O'Ferrall from its PR department for the first month, to give you a hand. It might be a good idea to have a run up to their offices at Awali to meet him beforehand.'

Bapco – or, to give it its formal name, the Bahrain Petroleum Company, a subsidiary of Caltex – was headquartered in its own purpose-built township right in the middle of the island, an oasis of picket fences, trees, greenery and everywhere the tinkle of hoses watering the grass, a little piece of Middle America in the heart of the Arab world. Bahrain was the first country in the Gulf where oil was discovered, through the tireless prospecting and optimism of a New Zealander, Major Frank Holmes. The state was then a British protectorate but no British company had been prepared to take the risk and the concession was taken up by an American group. Well No 1 gushed oil in 1932 and changed the face of the Gulf for ever.

The prefabricated houses of Awali were built in the 1940s, large, medium or small according to the rank of the occupier, and had been intended as only temporary. Thirty years on, they were still there, air-conditioned, comfortable and seemingly indestructible.

Jim walked into the reception area to greet me. Softly-spoken, small, with silver-rimmed spectacles to match his already silver hair, this veteran newspaperman was to prove a staunch ally and a firm friend, a fount of wisdom and an unflagging source of help. 'I think we need a beer. We'll nip round to my house.' As we walked round to the parking area, this was to be one of those defining moments of truth. Four young children, a man in his late forties, I mused, I suppose we're talking second-hand Hillman saloon. We walked along a row of cars and paused at a gleaming new Mercedes. 'Hop in,' said Jim.

The budget of the *Gulf Mirror* had included a small amount to provide a car and I had duly taken delivery, again through a branch of the Al-Moayyeds, of an air-conditioned Datsun, not the smallest, but by no means the largest either. Perfectly serviceable, indeed comfortable, but a Mercedes it was not. At that moment it began to dawn on me that the money I was being paid as editor, some £3,000 a year, admittedly tax-free, might not be as generous as I had thought, even though it was double my salary in England.

Inside the house, Jim's slim, elegant Irish wife Elizabeth brought in the beers on a tray as we discussed content, upcoming stories, Bapco's support and the sheer logistics of producing an English language newspaper in Arabia. 'It's going to be tough,' he cautioned. 'I know these buggers.' He had been referring to the printing press but his words, I was to find, would also encompass the wide range of dramatis personae that I was to come into contact with. On a clear horizon that sunny winter's day, it was a tiny dark cloud. Nothing to worry about, I thought.

CHAPTER FOUR

The round of introductions, handshakes and endless cups of Arabic coffee went on as I continued to meet the people who would play a part in producing the newspaper. With Belgrave I walked into the centre of the town, to a small shop on the edge of the suq, its window crowded with books, framed by the steel roller shutters that every trader deemed it prudent to have. 'This is Anwar Abdul-Rahman,' he said as, inside, a youthful figure in western clothes came towards us. The dapper Anwar, exuding energy, was to be a key player, taking charge of distribution and circulation. There was nothing, I was to find, that he did not know about publishing, or politics, or business, or indeed poetry and literature. Anwar, with slick dark hair and a side parting, knew everyone; years later, he was a multi-millionaire, having built up a publishing and print empire in Bahrain with newspapers and magazines of a quality that rivalled any in the world. He was cheery, witty, and wise. I left his little bookshop with a renewed confidence.

Back to Awali, there to meet the man who was to become the *Gulf Mirror*'s freelance photographer. Abdulla Khan, trained and employed by Bapco, was to prove a find. In a crisp white shirt and razor-creased black trousers, his shy smile was deceiving: he was a born professional cameraman, tireless, dedicated and reliable, whose brilliant work was to enhance the pages of the paper.

We needed a woman columnist. Jim More O'Ferrall, who had led me to Abdulla Khan, took me to meet Shay Sawyer, a zany character who stood out among the more staid residents of Awali. Shay, barely into her thirties, of Irish origin, long dark brown hair in ringlets, slim and petite, had lived in the township for more than ten years. She already had a reputation as a talented writer.

She was hesitant at first, there were other commitments, not to mention a busy social life and bridge, and looking after her two children. I eventually managed to persuade her. We shook hands, and she roared off in her grey Austin-Healey Sprite, the battered two-seater sports car vanishing in a cloud of exhaust fumes.

The help of Bapco's Ali Shihaab was also enlisted, to write masterly articles on aspects of life in Bahrain, the clarity of his meticulously crafted exposition drawing praise from the local head of BP, Peter Stirling, in a published letter to the paper.

'You're going to need a hand with the general coverage,' said Jim, as we relaxed later over cigars and coffee at his home. 'You can't do it all on your own, and I know the very man. As a matter of fact, he's hoping to hear from you. He's a former British foreign correspondent, based here, working as a stringer for the *Financial Times* and for Agence France Presse, and frankly, he needs the money. He lives in a traditional Persian house in Manama's old quarter. I'll arrange for you to meet.'

Early that evening, walking through the street, directions scrawled on the back of an envelope, wind raising the loose sand so that it stung my eyes, I spotted the old studded door of weathered teak, framed in a tiny entrance porch. Next to it was a stained white bell push, wires barely concealed.

I could hear footsteps shuffling along a passage, then the door opened. Stooping, there was Ralph Izzard, hand outstretched in welcome, now turned sixty, spare and lean . . . and with a parrot on his shoulder. He gestured. 'This is Charlie.' The African grey looked back, unblinking.

Inside, the passage led to an open courtyard of white-washed walls, with a cushion-strewn stone bench running alongside a strip of garden where plants struggled; narrow poles stuck out of the side of the old house; from one dangled the parrot's cage. Off the open area was a small dimly-lit majlis, with faded, threadbare kilim rugs.

With Ralph leading the way, we passed through the first courtyard and down stone steps into a small sunken garden ringed by palms, the golden shoots of the new date crop already visible. To one side, charcoal glowed in a hearth as a barbecue of Australian steaks was in preparation. A hose in one of the flower beds gushed water from the island's subterranean supply. 'My dear chap,' said Izzard, 'have a drink. Whisky-water? Or a cold Tuborg?'

The house, faded and worn, had seen better times, but its charm remained. It was spacious yet intimate, and its tiled floors were cool in summer – and cooler still in the Gulf's often uncomfortably cold winters. It was one of the few left in the city to have a Persian wind tower, a cleverly devised structure split into quarter segments by vertical diagonal panels, designed so that, in the height of summer, through the airless nights, whatever slight breeze there was would be caught, from any direction, and wafted down one of the shafts, providing some slight relief from the humid, enervating airlessness that enveloped the sleeper like a damp flannel. And it still would, without the blessings of the air-conditioners that almost everyone, rich and poor, operated in their homes.

Off the courtyard, the bedroom doors bore polished, ornate brass fittings and massive hinges. There was an occasional trickle of soil inside the rooms where faded red mangrove poles, brought in by dhow from Mombasa and Dar-es-Salaam, supported the ceiling and an earth roof. The palm fronds in the garden rustled, stirred by a puff of wind; it was already sundown, and the soft velvet of a Gulf night approached. Above our heads, a panoply of stars appeared one by one. Our own planetarium.

The evening wore on, the slow murmur of Ralph's conversation, reminiscences and anecdotes accompanied by the rustle of the robe of his Omani servant, Abdulla, as he moved to and fro, the scurrying of tree rats, unseen, and the clink of the ice in our glasses. After a lifetime in the trouble spots of the world, in a career that began in the offices of the *Daily Mail* in Berlin, in Nazi Germany, Izzard had at last found a safe haven. The Arabs, recognising an eccentric, treated him with tolerance and a warm affection, an affection that Izzard, ever the professional newspaperman, was happy to capitalise on.

As the wine was poured, the minarets surrounding the old house one by one burst into voice, the sing-song chanting tones of the different muezzins each distinctive and recognisable: 'In the name of God, the Compassionate, the Merciful, no other God but Allah, and Mohamed is his Prophet.' And from outside came scurrying steps as the faithful headed for the mosques and evening prayers.

'Well, covering stories is no problem, old boy,' drawled Izzard. 'Been doing that all my life and I could do with some extra work.' Indeed he could, with the upkeep of a rambling Georgian mansion in Tunbridge Wells to fund, occupied by his authoress wife Molly and two of his four children. 'But what I'd really like to do would be to write a column. Never done that before. Always fancied it.' I hadn't thought of that but readily saw the two-for-one economies, as it were. It was agreed. Reporter and writer. 'But I can't start until the middle of January,' he warned. 'I've got some filming commitments.' Among his retainers was one for the London-based film group Viz News, which sent him off, packing a heavy cine camera, anywhere in the Gulf and Oman where a story came to light. Damn, I thought, he'll miss the first couple of issues. Can't be helped. I've got Jim to cover, even if it is only for one month.

The visit also solved another problem: where to find a proof-reader. It turned out that his lanky and languid son, Miles, in his early twenties, then staying with him on an extended visit, could also do with some gainful employment. I left the old house, pleasantly full of steak, beer and red wine, and with a reporter, columnist and proof-reader added to the still unborn newspaper's complement. Perhaps we really were getting there.

But pulling it all together rested on me and the primitive printing works. Yet there's no denying that things always take on a more rosy glow after drink is taken. And drink had been taken. It oiled the wheels of that first meeting, and most editorial meetings with Izzard thereafter. Not for nothing was Ralph a great traditionalist.

CHAPTER FIVE

The team was now in place. All we had to do was to produce the newspaper. Issue number one. That meant stories, the usual pre-publication wishlist that faces every editor: page leads, second leads, features, fillers, and, of course, a design. As this was to be a first, it had to be something special. What better than a message from His Highness the Ruler? I approached Belgrave.

He came back two days later, remarkably quickly for a country where time sometimes seemed to stand still. 'His Highness thinks it would be more appropriate if his son the Heir Apparent welcomes this new publication.' He muttered some PR-speak about the need to raise the profile of Sheikh Hamed, a clean-cut, athletic and charismatic Sandhurst product, currently in the United States, later to become Ruler, and then King. 'What would you like him to say?' 'Leave that to me, James.' I hurriedly hammered out a few words on my little portable typewriter. They were approved by the palace without change.

That took care of the formalities, but we still needed stories. Jim, ever the seasoned newspaperman, and with sixteen years' experience of living in Bahrain with his ear to the ground, started hitting the phone. I also had my own list of tip-offs gleaned from drinks parties, as usual jotted on the back of an envelope. I left the office to track them down, drawing heavily on the goodwill created by a charm offensive of the previous few days to overcome the suspicions, if not downright hostility, that characterised many of the island's jobsworth Britons, cosy in their sheltered taxfree haven where everyone knew their place, or certainly should do. For them, Bahrain was a largely middle-class replica of Surbiton, even with its own golf club.

First stop was the imposing seafront office of Gray, Mackenzie, with an anchor and flagpole adorning the gravelled forecourt, a suitable image for the Gulf headquarters of a shipping group with a proud colonial past and still moving only cautiously into a modern world. There were high stools in the lower office which bustled with Indian clerks, but I did not notice a quill pen. I am sure they were there, in the stationery store.

Donald Orde, the general manager, greeted me in his large office. Neat, spruce, outwardly cautious, he was also wary, like welcoming a newcomer wearing suede shoes into the members' lounge of the Madras Club. This was to have been an interview, but it turned out to be an interrogation. Of me. Aware of safety in numbers, Orde had brought in his big guns: his deputy, Jim Kergan, a bristling little man, and his Number Three, Ian Malcolm, with slicked-back prematurely grey hair and a deep perma tan from years spent east of Suez as a servant of the company.

'Delighted,' said Malcolm as he held out his hand. 'Just back from Scotland myself, a spot of leave. Do you stalk?' That almost threw me. 'Only rarely.' There they sat, each questioning me on my background, trying to sum up my credentials. I tried to weather this unexpected squall with a feigned naivety and innocence. They decided that perhaps they liked me after all.

What I wanted from them were details of a big new expansion by the group, to run a large number of deep-water berths planned by Dubai, the bustling, go-ahead sheikhdom further down the Gulf. Gray Mack, as it was known, would take overall charge of the new dock, Port Rashid, providing harbourmaster, tugs and docking services. This Arab version of a great leap forward would take the pocket-handkerchief-sized state out of the dhow age, where a fleet of sturdy ocean-going wooden boats still used the Creek, a huge inner lagoon, to load and unload their cargoes, and into the big league. It would also prove the foundation for a future that would one day eclipse Bahrain. The almost paranoid suspicion with which the Bahrainis viewed their upstart cousins would have gone into overdrive, had anyone made the connection. They didn't. I left my audience with the Three Wise Men – or should it have been the Three Brass Monkeys – with my notebook crammed with facts, figures, time scales and projections.

Back in the office, as I started to type up the story, Jim had also come up trumps. 'I've found out that Cable & Wireless are going to slash phone bills by 40 per cent with a new cheap period for calls. That's a page lead.' 'Page lead?' I spluttered. 'It sounds like the bloody splash.' And it was. By a stroke of luck, at the very start of the week we had our main front page story. Things were gathering pace.

As half of our readership would be women, I reasoned, we needed a strong feminine slant. Again, Jim came to the rescue. 'There's a friend in Awali who's just won a top prize in a BBC worldwide competition with her recorded account of how her three sons survived a terrorist hijack of a British Airways VC10.'

Virginia Hatcher's boys, on their way back to boarding school in England complete with pet terrapin, were held hostage with other passengers on Dawson's Field in Jordan before their release was negotiated. Pictures of the aircraft being blown up by their Palestinian captors were beamed to television audiences world-wide. Virginia, thirty-four, a pretty brunette who worked as a broadcaster for Awali's radio service, later recorded her recollections of those nail-biting moments as she and her husband, a power engineer, sat at home for hour after long hour waiting for news. That took care of our first interview on the 'Feminine Focus' page.

From Ahmed Suleiman, the gravel-voiced announcer with Radio Bahrain, came an account of the Ruler's recent visit to a snow-covered Teheran, sealing the end of a bad-tempered stand-off with the giant neighbour across the water which had lasted years, until the Shah, later to be deposed in a bloodless coup, dropped his claim to Bahrain's borders. The chain-smoking Suleiman, a Palestinian, veteran broadcaster and the local stringer for Reuters, was to prove a staunch friend who could always be relied upon to supply column inches.

We needed more. I picked up a gold-edged invitation card on my desk. 'Who's this from?' 'From Jean Thuillier, catering manager of Gulf Aviation,' explained Jim. 'One helluva character. You're honoured – it's for his New Year's Day party which has become something of an institution.' And it made the back page lead.

Channel Islander Thuillier, wine expert, restaurateur, raconteur and bon viveur at once delightfully charming and rudely abrasive, was a man of many talents. He was to become the paper's culinary writer, reporting from all over the world during his annual six-week 'busman's holiday' for his highly individual column, 'Travels with Thuillier'.

At the party, three hundred guests crammed the rooms of his colonial-style wood-beamed apartment. Plus a British regimental band, a Welsh male voice choir, and a traditional five-man group of Bahraini musicians with hand-held drum, piping trumpet and stringed instruments. The highlight was the appearance of Thuillier dressed as the Pope. The noise was indescribable. One guest, a burly naval officer, turned to me. 'Now I know what it was like to be a stoker at the Battle of Jutland.'

But the week was running out; it was already Thursday. Then, mannah from heaven: a labour dispute that had halted the building of the huge aluminium smelter in the desert had finally been peacefully resolved, after 17 days, following the intervention of Jawad Al-Arrayed, the smartly-dressed British-trained lawyer who was the head of labour affairs for the government. Over coffee in his office he readily supplied me with full details, at a meeting that was to mark the start of a close friendship. Arrayed, in turn amusing, irascible, cultured and down to earth, who years later steered Bahrain to victory in a bitter legal battle with neighbouring Qatar to have Bahrain sovereignty of the Hawar Isles confirmed, was to become a deputy prime minister. He was a man who did not suffer fools gladly and I was to sorely try him, over the years.

In our gossip column, 'People and Places', we had colourful coverage of the wedding of Khaled Zayani, scion of one of the island's merchant princes. We were full, apart from the necessary two-paragraph fillers – and the soccer results which would come in over the Reuters wire late on Saturday evening.

The stories were written and some were already typeset – Miles Izzard was hard at work proof-reading and I was toiling with ruler, pencil and rubber, designing the pages on large, newspaper-sized ruled sheets, my desk littered with photographs, discarded Reuters stories, empty bottles of Pepsi and an ashtray overflowing with the butts of cheroots. But we had yet to see one complete page proof. 'I think it's time to investigate,' said Jim. I headed out of the office, down the street and up the litter-strewn back alley that led to the door of the press.

The next day, Friday, was traditionally the Muslim holy day when all work stopped. At the press it was continuing – but on other newspapers. A small handful of galley proofs hung from a nail marked 'Gulf Mirror'. I could see a pile of copy on the desk. My copy, and clearly untouched. 'It's going well,' said Matthew, disarmingly.

At my cajoling, nay insistence, he reluctantly agreed to produce a proof of one entire page, ordering an Indian worker to stop working on an Arabic publication. He began to assemble the different columns of type from the random, where typeset work is deposited, working from the corrected proofs I had supplied. He slowly and carefully inserted the new lines of type, tossing the old ones on the floor, and then began filling up one of the steel 'chases' into which the various stories and headlines would be locked. An hour later I was still waiting, building up what could fairly be described as a head of steam. Kipling's words were at that time unknown to me: ' . . . a fool lies here who tried to hustle the East'. Even if they had been, they would have been of scant comfort.

Finally, I bore the smudged page proof back to the office.

Triumph would be the wrong word; despair perhaps a little closer. 'I warned you,' said Jim. 'They'll break your heart.' One down, only eleven more to go for this first issue. At this rate, we'd be lucky to produce it in time for January 10, never mind the 3rd. It had been a foretaste. The day went on. Two more page proofs appeared, were laboriously tweaked and corrected, and signed off. I collapsed into my office chair. Tomorrow was press day and with butterflies in my stomach, I felt myself on the eve of an epic battle; Waterloo sprang to mind. I had an awful feeling that I might be cast as Napoleon.

I was back in the office at 8.30 the next morning. Operations at the press were in full swing – on other papers, I couldn't help noticing. But the pace did seem to be quickening. Proofs came and went, lunch was taken at our desks, and more pages were corrected, finished and signed off. The proofing process still seemed to take an eternity but as the afternoon wore on, progress seemed – I hardly dared hope – even encouraging.

At 5.30 I called a break. 'I really think,' I said to Jim, 'that we're going to get out of here by about nine o'clock.' His words were ominous. 'I wouldn't be too sure. I know these bastards.'

As dusk fell swiftly, I began to feel that I was entering the heart of darkness. Ten o'clock came and went. Still much to do. The clock in the overseer's office showed midnight. Fikhri, the paste-up artist, had been working without a break, breathing heavily, sucking his stained teeth as he sliced and cut and stuck, meticulously, carefully and oh so slowly.

He was joined at his desk by his beautiful young Egyptian wife, doe-eyed and with flawless café au lait skin. She started glancing at me nervously, fidgeting more and more as the hours wore on. One o'clock. Two o'clock. Tears filled her eyes and slowly rolled down her cheeks as she wept noiselessly. I knew how she felt.

At three o'clock and four o'clock I was beyond tears. Then, at last, we were on the final page, the front. Fikhri worked on, cigarette drooping from his lip. 4.40: one last headline to be stuck.

GULF WEEKLY MIRROR

Telephone : Manama 4324

Sunday January 3, 1971. NO. 1   PRICE 100 FILS BAHRAINI, 1 QDR, 75 FILS KUWAITI.

CUT IN PHONE TOLLS

CABLE and Wireless have cut telephone charges by up to 40 per cent in a new cheap period for subscribers in Bahrain.

Cheaper phone calls started for Bahrain on New Year's Day. There are two systems of charging, the company's regional manager, Mr. L. C. Hill, explains.

Either the subscriber chooses the existing "person to person" service — with a reduction in the time for every minute after the first minutes.

Or a new cheaper "number to number" service where charging begins from the time the number answers — with reduced rates throughout the call.

Also there are cheaper rates from 7 p.m. to 7 a.m. and all day Friday, which apply to both services.

This last concession means a reduction of about 40 per cent below the full daytime rate and that for the full 36 hours from 7 p.m. on Thursday evening to 7 a.m. on Saturday morning, the telephone can be used at the lower charge.

Only drawback about the new "number to number" service is that the subscriber needs to be sure the person he wants to speak to is at the other end. If that person is out, and someone else answers the caller must pay.

The reductions have been made possible by using new and improved techniques of communication, particularly the tropospheric scatter stations, one on top of the Jebel and one near Isa Town, which link Bahrain with Dubai and the Trucial States, and with Qatar respectively.

Cable and Wireless investment in these stations and other important new advances in communications technology meant both a more efficient and a cheaper service, with the benefits being passed on to subscribers said Mr. Hill.

Future plans include a subscriber dialling service which will make it as easy to dial Abu Dhabi, Dubai, or Doha as it is in Muharraq or Jezra. This service may possibly be introduced in two years' time.

Once subscribers have become used to the direct dialling system around the Gulf, it is intended to extend the service worldwide.

And one further development on the way is the "typewriter" telephone — a numbered keyboard instead of a dialling disc. This will at first be used by operators and later be made available to private subscribers, but not for at least two years.

Cable and Wireless have also announced the setting-up of a direct telegraph link with Iran.

MESSAGE FROM HEIR APPARENT

His Excellency the Heir Apparent, Shaikh Hamed bin Isa Al Khalifah, has sent the following message to the Gulf Mirror.

It gives me great pleasure to welcome this first issue. A weekly English newspaper in Bahrain, to circulate both on our Islands and throughout the Gulf, is something for which there has long been a need.

It will serve not only as a vital news medium for all the people on Bahrain, but also as a record for charting the progress of the many companies, both in commerce and industry, as our economy continues its surge ahead.

And in addition it will also provide a useful guide to the many social and leisure events each week. I praise the initiative of the Bahraini businessmen behind the project and wish the Gulf Weekly Mirror every success.

Snow hits the F.A. Cup ties

HOLDERS Chelsea were given a fright by London rivals Crystal Palace in a see-saw draw as the wintry weather cut into the third round of the English F.A. cup yesterday.

Snow and ice forced the postponement of ten of the 32 ties, but there was no shortage of excitement at Palace's Selhurst Park ground where a 42,000 crowd saw Chelsea snatch a late equaliser through Tommy Baldwin.

Shocks were rare, but fourth division York City trimmed Second Division Bolton Wanderers 2-0 and Scunthorpe United, also of the Fourth Division, forced a goalless draw away to first Division West Bromwich Albion.

Swansea City, 6-1 winners against non-league Rhyl, and Wolverhampton Wanderers, 5-1 conquerors of Norwich City, were the top scorers.

Wolverhampton, one of the favourites to win the trophy, looked in trouble as they struggled to a 1-1 half-time score against Norwich. But the Wolves produced a four-goal second half blitz with Jimmy McCalliog and Bobby Gould both scoring twice.

First Division Nottingham Forest were held to a 1-1 draw by Second Division Promotion Challengers Luton Town.

NEW STAMPS FOR DUBAI

Dubai has issued a new set of stamps to commemorate development projects in the state.

The five stamps ranging in value from 60 dirhams to five Riyals show the new 224 million sterling Port Rashid, the new Dubai International Airport, the 300 — bed Rashid Hospital under construction by Bernard Sunley, the tall National Bank of Dubai building beside the creek and the Dubai Trade School.

NAVAL RATING DROWNS

DEATH by misadventure was the verdict of a court of inquiry into the death of Mechanical Engineer 1st Class John Roderick MacGregor whose body was found beneath Mina Sulman Jetty on Tuesday morning. MacGregor, from Glasgow, was serving aboard the minesweeper HMS "Beachampton".

Issue number one: toil, tears and sweat marked the birth of the *Gulf Mirror*

Then the completed page was borne off to the camera room for the last plate to be made. It was all over.

'Congratulations,' said Jim. 'You've done it! The southern Gulf's first English language newspaper. I can't believe it. Well done.'

But I was beyond any feelings of success. We retired to the nearby Delmon Hotel for coffee and breakfast; as I visited the Gents' to freshen up I was in such a state of exhaustion, utterly drained, that as I turned to wash my hands I nearly thrust them into one of the wall-mounted urinals.

That night was my first taste of a printing purgatory. It can only get better, I thought.

CHAPTER SIX

There was barely time after my dawn breakfast for a brief shave in my room at Ralph's house, where I had now been billeted, when I was back on the road, to the airport where my wife Christine was flying in from London on a VC10 with our two young daughters. The jet touched down on time at 7am and my daughters scampered past police and immigration officers to jump into my arms. Behind followed Chris, slim, blonde and with her cheerfulness and good humour intact despite a sleepless flight looking after two energetic children.

The car swung out from the airport car park and on to the dusty road, past the dusty minarets, dusty houses and dusty palm trees. I coughed nervously. 'This is something special,' said Christine. 'Just how I imagined it to be.' A surprise reaction, after our experience of the vibrant colours of East Africa. Initial impressions always count. She never changed her view. Her first question was: 'What's our house like?' 'Fine darling, but we're staying for a few days with Ralph, while things are sorted out.' God forgive me.

I led the family upstairs to our rooms; massive wooden beds, old brass Persian candlesticks on the windowsills, wooden shutters, and already the gathering bustle of life outside as the Bahrainis moved to and fro across the sandy square as another day began. We all climbed into the beds, sheets still damp from the Bahraini winter which was to give me uncomfortable backache for days. Three hours later, the excitement of arriving in a strange foreign country proved too much and the family were up and ready for breakfast. 'How long are we staying here?' asked Christine. Just a little while, I assured her. But she was always perceptive. 'There isn't a house, is there?' she asked. 'Well, not right this minute, no,' I said, and recounted the story of the one that got away, and the various totally unsuitable flats that I had been encouraged to rent. Not a good beginning. But within three months, through some sleight of hand and not a little help from the Ruler, we would be in one of the most modern houses currently being built.

That afternoon we toured the main island, taking in Awali, the oil company's beach complete with pier at Zallaq, on the west coast, and the gardens of Budaiya on the fertile north-eastern coastal strip, and then back for afternoon tea at the dazzlingly white new Gulf Hotel on the edge of Manama, just opened, five stars, and where rooms could hardly be had for money, let alone love, even in a wealthy Arab sheikhdom.

As a tour, it had been a success, but there still hung over us the vexatious question of a house. The newspaper's board had restricted me to a monthly budget of around 170 Bahraini dinars, somewhere approaching £160, by no means adequate to secure the standard of home we had been used to. That sort of money would mean a gloomy apartment in a paint-peeling block, concrete as usual cracked, battered windows; there were dozens of these sub-standard blocks, used to house the overflow of British service families whose complaints did not matter to the military machine; rents even then were exorbitant, and I felt smug delight when, only two or three years later, Bahrainis protested angrily to me at the soaring prices of London property when they went in search of investment for their new-found petrol dollars as the price of oil rocketed.

The board of the *Gulf Mirror* was a hybrid, made up of the great and good and not so good. Each had invested a thousand dinars, more out of a sense of public duty than a serious commitment; one did not even pay his contribution for months, until he could be sure the paper would not sink without trace. They were, largely, good men who, having stumped up what to them was petty cash, had no wish to be troubled by the minutiae of running a little business; but others did indeed have their own agenda and were to prove a thorn in my side.

The law of Bahrain decreed that a newspaper had to have, in addition to its editor, a 'responsible editor' who could be conveniently sent to prison if content was to give more than the usual offence to the government. That role was filled by Ebrahim Eshaq, of an old Persian family and owner of a prosperous furnishing store, in addition to myriad interests, property and otherwise. Eshaq, dapper, slim, carefully groomed hair and immaculately dressed in English suits, controlled the budget. He made it quite clear that the sum allotted for my accommodation was not negotiable. The day was saved, for the moment, by Derek Fletcher, the local partner of a British firm of chartered accountants, Whinney Murray. Fletcher, a portly Pickwickian figure, bustling, cheery and brimming with bonhomie, rang me. 'Hear you're having a bit of trouble with housing, old chap. I can help out. We've got a nice house that has just become vacant and you're welcome to have it for two or three months, until you find your feet.'

Saved by the bell, I thought, as we moved to the detached single-storey luxury home in its own garden, ringed by date palms and with oleander bushes lending a splash of colour. The children explored as Christine scurried through the kitchen, her progress punctuated with bangs from the heel of her shoe as she despatched fleeing cockroaches. Our temporary home was the venue for a party weeks later to celebrate the first ten issues of the Gulf Mirror. Coloured lights ringed the garden as the scores of guests arrived, with those first issues of the paper proudly displayed along one wall. Sheikhs, ministers, government officials, company presidents and captains of industry and their wives poured in, and of course most of the newspaper's directors. The drinks flowed, canapés supplied by the catering section of Gulf Aviation were irresistible, and the evening was judged a great success. But not by Eshaq, who grumbled loudly when he saw the invoices. He would have grumbled even more had he known that the drinks bill concealed two boxes of Havana cigars for myself.

The weeks at our house passed quickly and happily, but I knew that it could only be a short-lived idyll. Then again, luck rode to the rescue in the form of an English friend in the island's Special Branch, who knew I was still looking for a permanent home. 'I know a merchant who's building a lovely house down the road,' he told me over a beer. 'I'll have a word and fix up a meeting.' The landlord, who sold clothing material in the suq, was a sly, greedy little man whose face remained inscrutable. The monthly rent was 200 dinars, no negotiation. I returned to him several times. He was impassive, take it or leave it. 'I'll take it,' I told him. He arranged for the tenancy agreement to be drawn up, an impressive document in Arabic bearing the head of the Ruler at the top. Money up-front, of course. I took it to the company secretary, Malcolm Wrightman, the highly qualified and public-spirited Anglo-Indian who ran one of the sheikhdom's most successful businesses for its Bahraini owner. 'You realise this means that you have to find the balance yourself?' he asked. He signed it on behalf of the newspaper. 'You will also need another signature, from Ebrahim Eshaq,' he warned. 'That may not be easy.' An understatement if ever there was one.

I delivered the document to Eshaq. He received it without comment. A week passed. 'I'm still looking at it,' he said. Another week went by. 'It's still with me.' At that point I had to make a fleeting visit back to London. I handed Christine the job of getting that vital signature. What followed, I later found, was a piece of high farce, and the outwitting of Eshaq. As she sat in his office, and he began to tell her that it was simply not possible for him to sign the two-year agreement, even though we were prepared to pay the difference, she lost her temper. His English secretary listened outside as she berated him. As he picked up the tenancy document, she snatched it from him . . . and quickly realised that it did not in fact need his signature. That of Wrightman was sufficient. As she stormed out, a blonde bundle of feminine fury, with Eshaq speechless, his office fell silent. The secretary later told me that it was one of the funniest moments she had ever witnessed.

That evening the merchant had his tenancy agreement, our cheque was paid over, and she had the keys. The house was beautiful; steps led from the wrought iron gate up to the front door, where there was an ample veranda; each interior doorway was richly inlaid with different types of wood; the flooring was of cool tiles, the inside stairway marble; a long balcony ran outside the main bedroom – there were three others; and upstairs, from the roof terrace, we had a view across the island to the palm-fringed sea in the hazy distance. The house still had to be furnished and a garden planted, and the purchase of six vital air-conditioner units was a major expenditure.

On my return from London, making my obligatory courtesy call on the Ruler, he asked about my housing problem. I mentioned the air-conditioners and how these threatened to outrun my own slender resources. 'I would like to buy them,' he said. 'Leave the address with me.' The units arrived a day later, still in their packing cases and, it must be said, top of the range.

Eshaq, ever the gentleman, accepted defeat magnanimously. 'When you buy your furniture, don't forget my store,' he said. 'I'll give you a good discount.'

CHAPTER SEVEN

Sometimes when I looked back to my previous life, it all seemed a world away. I had previously been chief sub-editor of a morning newspaper circulating throughout the North-East. The work was demanding, working through piles of copy at the beginning of the night, viewing the day's photographs, then deciding what we would lead on at the conference with the editor at six o'clock, before marking up the copy for distribution to my team of sub-editors; we were always short-staffed and the night, however dramatic the news might be, was a constant grind. I would leave the office at around 1.15 in the morning feeling wrung out, and return to our home in a picturesque village where it could take another hour for me to wind down from the constant adrenaline rush. The little village was idyllic and the garden into which I poured my off-duty hours a constant salve to my other life of night work.

But something was missing. After working for the *Daily Mail*, we had spent two years living in Nairobi, where I was on the staff of the *East African Standard*, and memories of that vivid, exciting and stimulating time refused to fade away. There had to be more to life than my current treadmill existence.

Fate came to the rescue in the form of a tiny classified advertisement at the bottom of a 'Situations Vacant' page in the journalists' trade magazine, the *UK Press Gazette*. The job ad was intriguing. It read:

EDITOR – BAHRAIN ENGLISH WEEKLY
Salary £3,000. Plus furnished air-conditioned accommodation
for editor and family and car allowance. Tourist class passages
paid London/Bahrain. Annual leave can be taken at the rate of

six weeks every eighteen months, passage paid Bahrain/London London/Bahrain. Contract to cover two years terminable by three months' notice on either side.

I discussed it with Christine who, like me, was feeling life in England was a little dull, with a husband she never saw in the evenings, and living on a barely sufficient salary that allowed for few luxuries. 'Why not?' was her response. 'It doesn't hurt to inquire.' My letter was in the post the next day. Then we waited. Three weeks later the reply dropped through the letterbox, inviting me to an interview at an address in Mayfair, London. But there was a problem; I was due to work the previous evening, and there was no one I could swap with. That meant just a few hours' sleep. I took the precaution of going to the local library where I found, wonder of wonders, a book published ten years previously on life in Bahrain, the only one there. And in the past week there had been a lengthy think-piece in one of the quality Sundays on politics in the Gulf area.

We had no car and there seemed no way I could get to the mainline station three miles away in time to catch the 9a.m. express Pullman to King's Cross. I hitched a lift to Darlington with the milkman. On the train I speed-read the book on Bahrain and then studied the newspaper article. On arrival in London I had amassed all I needed to talk authoritatively on subjects about which I knew nothing. I arrived at the address I had been given, an elegant house in a quiet tree-lined street off Park Lane. There was no brass plate outside, or anything to indicate the nature of any business. As I sat down in the reception area, I asked the girl behind the desk: 'What does this firm actually do?' 'We're a public relations consultancy,' she told me. The hairs on the back of my neck stood up; at that time, to just about every newspaperman, public relations was anathema, viewed as a convenient bolt-hole for those who had failed to make it in the real world of journalism. A bad start, I thought.

A buzzer sounded and the girl took me upstairs to a large room overlooking the street, watercolours of the Middle East on the wall, where a pleasant, studious and possibly slightly raffish man waited. He was, I later learnt, ex-Foreign Office. He briefly ran through my experience, then we talked about Bahrain, and I was able to comment at length, thanks to my crash course on the train. And for good measure added my thoughts on problems at the Buraimi oasis, in Abu Dhabi, currently exercising Bedu tribes; this time, the result of hastily reading the newspaper piece. He seemed impressed. 'The whole project of this new newspaper is being organised by our man in Bahrain, James Belgrave,' he said. 'I think you're the man we're looking for, and I think he'll like you. As far as I am concerned, you've got the job. You'll be hearing from us.'

The journey back North passed in a daze; I could hardly believe my luck. It seemed too good to be true. And it was. Lengthy correspondence followed with Belgrave. I drew up designs for the new tabloid newspaper and then, anticlimax. Belgrave wrote to me saying that plans to employ me had been withdrawn. The newspaper's board had got the offer of the secondment of a journalist from the sheikhdom's oil company. It was thank you and goodbye.

To have such a promising job snatched away when it was almost in my grasp was a bitter blow. It was, I was to find out, entirely typical of the modus operandi of Belgrave. I filed away the correspondence with a heavy heart. Then three months later, just as I had been offered a job with the BBC, out of the blue another letter arrived from Bahrain. It was from Belgrave. offering me the job again. The oil company had decided that it could not afford to lose the services of its employee for two years. Was I still interested?

He wrote: 'You must think our organisation a very odd one, but having written to you in July saying that we had made alternative arrangements, which I explained, I am now writing to ask if you would, after all, be available to take over the editorship and, if so, when.

'By way of explanation, in July we had the offer, out of the blue, for the loan of an ex-journalist who was working in the Bahrain Petroleum Company's PR department, to act as editor for the first nine months of the *Mirror*'s existence, to get it off the ground, the oil company paying all costs. The offer was in fact made by the president of the oil company. The board accepted, not without misgivings on some people's part.

'However, the offer had been made during the absence on leave of the official in charge of personnel and PR in the oil company who, on his return, pointed out to the president all the things that would not be done if the person in question was seconded to us. There was a lot of coming and going, and finally the oil company revised their offer to one of the editor being available for only two months.

'We thought in view of this we should revert to our original plan, subject, of course, to your still being interested. I hope this background goes some way towards explaining our behaviour and I hope very much you are still willing to come out here.'

It was with mixed emotions that I again took the train southwards to London, where I met Belgrave for the first time. He towered above me, pleasant, bumbling and oozing affability, full of apologies for the about-turn and wooing me with a charm offensive that included an expensive lunch at a nearby Mayfair restaurant. He confirmed the job and the start date: December 12. Back North I went, to brief Christine fully on events; she was sceptical, and rightly so. I weighed everything up; it wasn't promising, the organisation was clearly unreliable, and this did not bode well for any future that involved Belgrave. How right I was. It would be a calculated risk. I took a deep breath. 'I'll take the job,' I told a very concerned Christine.

I wrote to Belgrave accepting the offer, put in my resignation and also gave the hard word to the BBC, who were not pleased. The die was cast; it was game on. There was no acknowledgement from Bahrain. For weeks I heard nothing. As my period of notice from the most senior job I had ever had began to run out, they were the longest weeks of my life. Finally, after days spent waiting in vain for a letter, I managed to ring Belgrave's office, the call being patched through a line of telephone operators, including Saudi Arabia. He wasn't there. I tried several times. Then, in desperation, I managed to contact the company secretary of the newspaper's parent publisher. Malcolm Wrightman was the absolute antithesis of Belgrave, a meticulous, highly professional graduate of an American business school. He was concerned that I had heard nothing. His telegram arrived the next day: 'Confirm appointment on terms Belgrave's recent discussions.' That was all I needed. The relief was overwhelming. I was on my way. A hardly auspicious beginning. But whatever difficulties lay ahead, I resolved, I would overcome them.

CHAPTER EIGHT

The Bahrain group of main islands numbers six, 15 miles from the coast of Saudi Arabia on one side and a similar distance from Qatar on the other. The name itself means 'two seas', though there has always been confusion as to the precise meaning: whether this refers to the sea on either side, or to the sea and the many under-sea springs of fresh water bubbling to the surface which years ago were used by divers to replenish supplies for the pearling fleet.

The climate in the winter months is pleasant, light sun, cool nights, blue skies, and with a temperature from December to April ranging from 10–20° centigrade (50–69° fahrenheit). In January and February it could be quite cold in the mornings. There were days when my wife Christine would insist on an electric fire before getting out of bed. Summer was a different story: more than 40° centigrade with humidity in August as high as 85 per cent. And there are claims that the merciless sun can even hit 50° centigrade. The summer heat was something that all expatriates just had to learn to live with, with the help of air-conditioned homes and offices and, even in those early days, air-conditioned cars as well. Leaving home on an August evening to some function or other, it was quite common for my shirt to become saturated on the walk from the front door to my car.

One summer I had to make a quick trip up to Kuwait; I had left Bahrain on August 1, dripping from the humidity as I boarded the aircraft on the tarmac. We landed in Kuwait an hour later in the full glare of the mid-day sun, with the glass reading 115° fahrenheit – and no trace of humidity. After Bahrain, it was like stepping out into a spring day. Most years there would be rain, spasmodic and short-lived. After months of oven-like heat, that first sound –

Bong! – of a raindrop hitting the air-conditioner units that protrude outside from all rooms was nothing short of magical, a moment to be savoured. But, alas, one that could never be guaranteed.

The weather could also get unseasonally cold. Within living memory, Bahrain experienced frost and, at the water's edge, the sea froze. Scores of elderly people literally died of cold as the temperature plummeted. Among the merchants, long-john underwear came out, to be worn unseen under robes made from heavy worsted wool. But for low-income workers the same clothing had to suffice; during one rainstorm I found myself driving behind a truck on a main road, packed with labourers on their way to work, drenched to the skin as the rain bucketed down, clinging to each other, a pictured of wretchedness.

It was a country of extremes. The sometimes almost intolerable summer heat was almost forgotten in winter, with extra blankets on the bed. But at the height of the hot season, when I returned home from the printing press at 4am, I would climb the stairs, still dripping with sweat, and for one delightful moment place my hand on the bedroom door, from the outside. It would be cold, beautifully, deliciously cold, from the air-conditioner within. I would open the door and walk into a wall of chilled air, almost like plunging through a curtain of cold water. Instant relief.

The humidity in August was unrelenting. On my way to the airport for a 2.30am flight, I was drenched by the time I had stepped into the car, and dripping again as I walked from the car into the terminal. Then, again, a contrast as I boarded the British Airways jumbo to be met by icy cold air-conditioning. As I sat in my seat, soaked, I began to shiver uncontrollably. I asked the cabin steward for a blanket. 'Are you sick?' he inquired solicitously. 'No, but if I don't get a blanket now, I will be,' I told him through gritted teeth.

I briefly took up golf, playing on the sand course near Awali built and maintained by the oil company. My regular partner was Norman Harvey, the burly and irrepressible head of safety at the aluminium smelter. One weekend we had arranged a foursome, teeing off at 7am, hoping to beat the height of the August heat while catching what slight breeze there might be at the slightly elevated 18-hole course. The first nine holes completed, we repaired to the clubhouse for a couple of much-needed chilled beers. By the time we stepped out again to resume play, the heat had built up. We struggled over the new few holes, play becoming slower and slower as we fought dehydration. One of the course's natural hazards was an ancient burial ground, tiny upturned rocks acting as headstones, and very much out of bounds, even though it was next to a fairway. 'Are you going on?' I asked Harvey. 'No, I've had it,' he gasped. 'If I get into that graveyard, I'll never leave it.' Heat stopped play.

The largest island is Bahrain itself, 30 miles long and up to 10 miles wide, and with a population when I arrived of barely more than 100,000. A causeway links it to Muharraq and the international airport. And years after my arrival, a massive sea bridge was built to Saudi Arabia, heralding the birth of a motorway network and a seven-day-a-week influx of rich Saudis arriving in the less-strict Bahrain for shopping and relaxation.

Also belonging to Bahrain are the Hawar islands, a small archipelago south-east of the main island and close to Qatar, too close to comfort. Ownership was contested in bitter squabbles until the dispute was finally resolved years later, in 2001, when the International Court of Justice ruled in Bahrain's favour after skilful negotiating led by my friend Jawad Al-Arrayed, the British-trained Bahraini lawyer and government minister. These lonely, barren and rocky isles were inhabited only by a handful of fishermen and quarry workers, and a small police post, but they are thought to hold reserves of oil and natural gas.

Manama, the sheikhdom's capital, was a mixture of garish new buildings, colonial-style villas with shaded verandas and traditional houses built from blocks of coral with massive studded teak doors and, inside, plasterwork carved into intricate patterns, following designs centuries old. Similar architecture can be found in Andalucia, with a heritage of 800 years of Arab culture. Gardens and date palms flourished to the north of the island, sustained by the abundant artesian water which, hundreds of years ago, was channelled underground in the qanat system of irrigation, now in ruins. Because of its position halfway down the Gulf, Bahrain had been a centre of trade since ancient times and is believed by some archaeologists to be the site of the ancient kingdom of Dilmun, an important commercial centre. It was a magnet for marauding armies, Portuguese, Persian, Arab and Omani, the last of which was that of the Al-Khalifa dynasty, which has ruled since the late eighteenth century, bringing stability, peace and prosperity.

The Copper Age, around 3000 BC, was a period of note, yielding the site of the largest prehistoric cemetery in the world: 100,000 burial mounds to the north and west, all of them plundered. It was during this period that trade links were developed with the copper mines of Oman and, further afield, to the East, to bring to Bahrain the spices, timber and prized perfumes for which Arabia was to become famous – Shakespeare referred to 'all the perfumes of Araby' in one reference, in *Macbeth*. Buried beneath the sands are the remains of a major civilisation, and an entire city, from the Copper and Bronze Ages. Babylon and Sumerian writing in the Third Millennium BC refer to Dilmun, in the Gulf, known as the 'land of immortality' and a meeting place of the gods. More recently, one of the oldest Islamic relics in the entire Gulf is the mosque of the Suq-Al-Khamis, three miles from the capital, with its beautiful twin minarets. The mosque, dating back to the tenth or eleven century AD, has now been restored.

To the people of Arabia, Islam is much more than a religion. As the guidance provided by Allah, it rules state, law and society. In Bahrain, as with the whole of the Arab world, Islam is central to life and the devout Muslim can apply the principles enshrined in the Koran to almost every moment of his life. The five Pillars of Islam are five rules he must obey if he is to be saved on the Day of

Judgment: *shahadah*, the declaration of faith, *salah*, five compulsory daily prayers, *zakah*, the giving of alms, *sawn*, fasting during the holy month of Ramadan, and the *haj* – pilgrimage to Mecca.

The meaning of Islam is submission to the will of Allah as revealed to Mohamed, the last in a line of Prophets (which included Jesus Christ) by the Angel Gabriel. These revelations form the Koran, regarded as the transcript of a tablet preserved in heaven, on which is written all that has happened and all that will happen – the authoritative word of Allah. In the Koran, all humans are equal before Allah, who judges them by their deeds, for which they will be held accountable. But Allah is merciful and compassionate, stated repeatedly in the Koran (the Arabic word means 'the recital') and humans are born pure and innocent.

The Koran was first revealed during Ramadan, which is why it is a holy month. The last and holiest night is the 27th – the Night of Destiny. Muslims believe that on this night there is a spiritual bridge between heaven and earth. 'In this night the angels of the Spirit descend to earth with the permission of Allah to settle all things. Peace accompanies this night until the break of day,' says the Koran. The end of Ramadan is marked by the Eid al Fitr, a day of family rejoicing and a national holiday, with feasting and celebration.

But Bahrain has always displayed great tolerance to non-believers. For many years there has been a Jewish community, well respected by other merchants, and set up by those fleeing persecution further north. And there are large Anglican and Roman Catholic churches which are a major part of expatriate life.

Bahrain has been a melting pot for different races. The original inhabitants were known as the Baharna, believed to be descended from the Arabs taken by Nebuchadnezzar into what is now Iraq. These people, Shias, fled from there to Bahrain, living mainly in the villages. Most of the Sunnis came to the island in the 18th century onwards, among them the ruling Al-Khalifa family. Then there are the Bahrainis of African descent, whose forebears were either slaves or freed slaves. Persians also settled in Bahrain and their cultural influence is seen in the fine old houses with wind towers.

The Bahraini is tolerant, warm and generous, and his hospitality unstinted. To welcome a caller into his home is not only an honour, it is an obligation – even if there has been a history of enmity with the guest. Crime is low, and usually petty.

The arts, poetry, music and painting, have always flourished and two of the leading artists were Karim Al-Arrayed, who specialised in local scenes, the suq, coffee houses and scenes from Manama and the coast, and Abdullah Muharraqi, whose Cubist-style pastiches in oil won him a reputation as Bahrain's own Picasso; his colourful work, drawing on island culture and incorporating pearl divers, pearls and palms, would be snapped up. One week Christine, after witnessing the dramatic street scenes at the Shia festival of Muharram, had the brainwave of commissioning a special work from Karim Al-Arrayed showing the marchers, all swirling banners and vivid robes. She made the mistake of mentioning this to Jawad Al-Arrayed when he next called at our home. When she went to collect the painting she was met by the artist with a long face. Jawad, a fellow Shia, had got there before her; the painting was now his. The next time she visited his home with the children, there was a space on his wall where the picture had hung; Jawad, it seemed, had hidden it under a bed. Thwarted yes, but Jawad was too nice a person for her to hold any resentment. She wrote it off to experience. We never did get another.

The history, life and times of Bahrain deserve a chapter to themselves. Bahrain was the first country outside the Arabian peninsula to be converted to Islam and the many ancient mosques, some dating back almost 1,000 years, testify to the island's devote adherence. The cultural background is equally impressive. One of the great Arabian poets of the early seventh century came from Bahrain and throughout history the archipelago has produced more writers and poets that its small size would suggest possible.

The first 'modern' school was founded in 1919 and the educational system, which grew from it, combined with scholarships for higher education overseas, provided educated men and women for commerce and industry, and to run the government's administration. Over the years Bahrain has advanced gradually and carefully, putting the island far beyond its neighbours for the greater part of the twentieth century; it is a story found in the Arabic Kalila wa Dimna, and also in Aesop's Fables, of the hare and the tortoise.

Long before the discovery of oil, Bahrain's fortune was founded on its natural resources. The most important was its supply of sweet water, both from artesian wells and from the springs that bubbled up under the sea and known to generations of pearling fleets. Without water, nothing can thrive. The palm tree was a source of raw materials for many trades in Bahrain in yesteryear. The fronds were used in the construction of fish traps all around the coast, and provided matting for the inside of dhows. Fronds were also used for making beds, mats, children's cradles, racks for utensils, even for a sort of hedging, for houses – the primitive barastis – and children's toys. Frond butts were used as floats attached to fishing nets. Ropes used in construction and as mooring lines for the dhows were woven from palm fibre. And most of all, the dates from the palm were an important staple food. Even today, to many local Arabs a meal would be incomplete without dates. The stones were used as fodder for cows and goats. During the season for fresh dates Bahrain is still self-sufficient, but hundreds of tons are imported from Iraq, Iran and Saudi Arabia for local consumption during the months when the many varieties are out of season.

Dates brought the need for both exports and imports, and thus the need for another industry, boatbuilding. Going back deep into history, Bahrain has always excelled in this, and many of the dhows were needed for pearling. They were built in a variety of places along the seashore, mostly around Manama, using teak planking brought from India. It was an industry that encompassed a major section of the population, from the merchants who imported the wood, the owners of the little yards, the shipwrights and the labourers who provided the variety of skills that went into creating a durable and seaworthy boat. Other materials also had to be imported: whale oil for treating the hulls, and whale fat for greasing the outer timbers below the waterline to make them watertight and to repel marine growth, caulking cotton, the heavy robust wooden block pulleys, and even the long masts.

In the building process, first the keel is laid down, and the stern and bow fitted. Then the ribs are fitted, and the sturdy planks nailed to them, going from bottom to top. Then comes the decking and other details. The work itself involved no modern equipment, just basic tools such as saws, hammers, adzes, and drills which were operated with a bow and string, much like the ancient method to create a spark from which to kindle a fire. The massive ocean-going dhows were all built with just these simple methods, and launched using the oldest power of all: manpower, to push the hull off the stocks to a point when it would plunge with a crash into the waters of the Gulf. There were a multitude of types, many of which died out with the arrival of modern steam-ships that could carry more cargo and faster. Two main types survived, the boom and the sambuk, for carrying freight and for fishing.

With the advent of cultured pearls in Japan, Bahrain's pearling industry went into decline, and boatbuilding with it. In 1835 an estimated 1,500 dhows sailed for the pearl beds; in 1971, there were just two. But the few remaining builders still turn out the tiny boats used every day to tend the fish traps: the jalbut (from which the Royal Navy term jollyboat derived), the huri and the balam, fitted with small diesel engines.

Closely related to boatbuilding is blacksmithing, practised for centuries in Bahrain. The island's blacksmiths supplied the shipwrights, using skills handed down from father to son. Coal was used for the forges which heated the scrap steel until it glowed red hot, when the smith can begin hammering it on his anvil, forming nails, bolts, rings, rudder hinges and anchors. As the hammer rose and fell, small boys worked the bellows, pumping the air continuously to keep the fires glowing.

Until the advent of cultured pearls, pearling had been the chief source of income for Bahrain and its neighbours, in an industry that involved thousands of people. The season, lasting from May to September, through the heat of the summer, drew a host of other nationalities to Bahrain to join the fleet. They arrived in hundreds from Persia, East Africa, from Socotra, part of an archipelago known as the Land of Sheba, off Yemen, and from closer to home, Saudi Arabia. Drawn by tales of the money to be made, even Bedu would leave their desert home to go to sea for the first time, joining the dhows setting sail from Bahrain. Some had never eaten fish before and many could not even swim. But there was a shortage of skilled manpower and the nakhodas – masters – had to take what they could, training them as the season advanced. There is an old story of how, when one of these recruits asked for a job, the nakhoda asked if he wanted to be a diver or a hauler. On being told that a diver earns twice as much, he said: 'May Allah make a diver out of me.'

Way back in 1835, the value of Bahrain pearls was thought to have reached £400,000. During the season, the fleets would be visited at sea by specialist merchants who dealt in pearls. They would return to Bahrain to sell them to bigger merchants who stayed on shore. These in turn would then voyage to India, the biggest market. Paris was also a major centre for the sale of pearls and in 1928 two Bahraini merchants became the first to travel there. They caused a disturbance when, realising it was time to pray, they took off their cloaks and knelt in one of the biggest squares. When they had finished, they stood up to find themselves surrounded by a curious crowd who had never seen anyone wearing Gulf clothes.

Gold and silver are other important commodities in Bahrain, worked and sold there ever since the island was settled. Necklaces, earrings, bracelets and rings are fashioned by Indian craftsmen in the suq, working at their benches behind the shops whose windows are lined with glittering displays to attract shoppers. They excelled at engraving silver and gold containers used as charm-carrying cases. In yesteryear Bahrain, these charms were common, and were worn round the neck or tied to the forearm to ward off evil spirits. The smiths also worked scabbards of swords and daggers in gold, inlaying them with pearls and precious stones. Both Manama and the island of Muharraq had their goldsmiths' districts and in Bahrain today, on the edge of the suq, there is a modern building housing many of these skilled artisans. Gold continues to play a major part in Bahrain's mercantile prosperity.

High-purity gold jewellery, usually 22 carat, has always been an important part of a Bahraini wife's daily wear, and western women too found their husbands could afford it, and began to adorn themselves with lavish displays. These found their way back to Europe and eventually to auction houses up and down Britain when expatriates returned home, back to the reality of a modest income once again, and needed to cash them in.

The list of ancient industries would not be complete without including cloth weaving, practised by the people of Bani-Jamra village, in Budaiya. For centuries they supplied the local market with woven material which was used for clothing, for the men's bishts and women's abbas, and also for sailcloth. Their cloth was even exported to Persia and to Qatif, on the Gulf coast of Saudi Arabia. But in the 1930s the industry began to decline as cheaper textiles were imported from Japan, only to experience a short-lived revival during the Second World War when trade with the

Far East abruptly ceased. When the war ended, imported textiles again started to find their way to Bahrain, from India as well as from Japan.

The cloth from the weavers of Bani-Jamra is made on primitive looms but could hardly be distinguished from products made elsewhere. The yarn was imported from India. some of it already dyed, though for many years they did the dying themselves. To produce cloth, the weaver sits in a small hut in the open air, with his legs dangling in a pit. The warps are stretched to the length required, secured to a stake way out in front of him on the open ground, and to a width of about a metre or more. A shuttle carries a ball of the weft and the weaver passes this to the left and to the right until half a metre is woven. Then he rolls the woven material on a wooden pin before him, and this process continues until the length of cloth is finished. Production is necessarily slow and painstaking, for only little reward, and this link with Bahrain's past was another dying industry when I arrived to launch the newspaper.

There was also weaving of another sort: to produce the mats found throughout the island which are woven from rush stalks. The type of rush used thrives in the marshy areas near Qatif. These rushes also grow in Bahrain but are not as high nor as good and supplies were brought to Bahrain by dhow. Sitra, on Bahrain's east coast and later a busy tanker port for the loading of oil from the Bapco refinery, was the home of this old craft and for years all the mosques and homes in Bahrain had mats made there.

To weave the mats, lengths of cords made from palm fibre are stretched to act as warps. Then between these cords the worker inserts the rush stalks breadthwise and closes them up using a hand loom. The left and right edges of the stalks are bent to the underside of the mat and cut to a uniform length. Mats made from rush have a bright yellow natural colour, and sometimes are tinted with vivid colours in attractive square patterns. They were popular and a long one, perhaps a metre wide by six metres, would be relatively expensive.

But again this was a craft slowly becoming extinct, both because of a shortage of craftsmen, with young people no longer interested, and because of the import of straw mats from China which were more compact and became more popular. In the 1950s there were a hundred people engaged in this work but their number gradually dwindled until by my arrival there were only about ten artisans kept busy.

One craft which has survived is pottery making, for which the inland village of Aali was famous. The earthenware jars, vases and containers for hubble-bubble pipes could be found in every home in Bahrain, sometimes fumigated by the burning of frankincense, brought from Salalah, in the south of Oman, and sold in the suq. The pottery is unglazed, but archaeological digs have uncovered coloured shards which suggest that glazed work may have been produced at one time. The clay is brought from Rifa'a and is in three main hues, brown, red and white, and each colour is used for different types of pots. First the clay is crushed to a powder, then moistened with water to become a paste. Then the potter takes a lump and throws it on his wheel, fashioning it into what-ever shape he wants. The result is put out in the sun to dry before being placed in the kiln to be baked. The pots are attractive but not robust; the nature of the clay makes them easily breakable which, like glassware, ensures continual repeat business.

The production of lime and gypsum still lives on and with construction booming when I arrived, demand soared with it. In the past, before the import of cement, most of the houses were built of stone, the blocks sealed in place using gypsum, and the exteriors plastered with lime. An example of this type of con-struction is the impressive old palace out in the desert at Sakhir, off the road to the coastal village of Zallaq, built using rocks from the sea. It was the home of an earlier ruler and when he died, according to tradition, his palace was abandoned. Years later, it was still intact, proof of the strength of this early form of building, shutters cracked and broken and banging in the wind, and its only occupants flocks of pigeons.

Today there is little call for sea rock but demand continues to be high for the lime which, like gypsum, is quarried in rock form in the desert and refined using kilns at Aali and near Sitra. After the burning, the rocks were once crushed using wooden flails and then sieved manually, before more mechanised methods were introduced. The resulting powder was poured into jute bags and sent to the market. These traditional methods were replaced by mechanised factories near Aali, kept busy producing lime for local builders. But gypsum is no longer used to hold stones together. It is prone to crumble because of the humidity, particularly in buildings near the coast, resulting in masonry becoming loose, and has been replaced by cement.

Bahrain's history, and the events that shaped its life, are well documented. In the time of Alexander the Great, when his fleet paid a peaceful visit in the third century BC, the main island was known as Tylos, and Muharraq was called Aradus, a name that has survived down the ages with the village of Arad. The sailors of Alexander were the first recorded tourists and as they travelled across the islands that make up today's Bahrain they noted that they were 'neither rugged nor woody but suitable for producing cultivated fruits and all things in due season'. They saw ancient ruins, possibly the host of burial mounds at Aali or the remains of the Barbar temple, which they thought were tombs of King Erythras, after whom the Gulf and the Arabian Sea were named in Greek times.

Little more was known of the history of Bahrain for several hundred years, until the seventh century AD, when Nestorian Christian writers described the large Christian community in Bahrain which it seemed had two bishops, one for the main island and the other at Masamig, now identified as Samahig, on Muharraq island. Bahrain's population, and also that of the

Arabian mainland, was made up of Christians, Jews, Zorastrians and pagans ruled by an Arab prince, Mundhir bin Sawa. When in AD 630 the Prophet Mohamed called on the neighbouring rulers including the Sassanid and Byzantine emperors and the Bahrain ruler to accept Islam, Mundhir was converted, as were many of his followers. And for the next three hundred years Bahrain was one of the provinces of the larger Islamic world owing allegiance to the caliphs who exercised their authority first from Mecca, and subsequently from Damascus and, under the Abbasids, from Iraq. The names of the early governors have been recorded and a number, such as Al-U'a Al-Hadrami, have become enshrined in the names of Manama streets. Caliphal rule was interrupted in the tenth century by an extreme sect, the Carmathians, who seized Bahrain and used it as a base for piracy that threatened the whole Gulf and much of Arabia. The whole eastern Arab world lived in fear of them, for they raided deep into Syria and Iraq and desecrated Mecca.

The fourteenth and fifteenth centuries were a time of turmoil, with various Arab maritime dynasties fighting for power in the Gulf. This period saw the emergence of the rocky Hormuz island, at the entrance to the Gulf, on the straits that carry its name, into a great trading centre described by travellers as the Venice of the east, despite its cruel and arid climate. Bahrain fell under Hormuz jurisdiction and when the Portuguese, the first Europeans to round the Cape, seized Hormuz and installed a puppet governor, they used the pretext of a non-payment of taxes to attack Bahrain and killed the ruler, Mukrim, after a long and bloody battle. This was in 1522, and although the Portuguese remained in Bahrain for another 80 years, these were turbulent times for the occupiers; they were never accepted by the islanders and governors were twice killed in rebellions. The huge fortress whose remains can be seen today on the east of the island, known as the Portuguese fort, was restored by the invaders but it had in fact been built much earlier, and underwent rebuilding in the seventh century AD; an inscription on Jidda island, which today houses a prison for long-term offenders, records the cutting at that time of the 100,000th block of stone for repairs.

Throughout its history Bahrain has been popular with visitors, from Alexander onwards, who have written about its people and resources. An early Arab traveller from Iraq, the merchant Sulman, described the island as he saw it in the ninth century; Idrissi, from Spain, wrote of it in the year 1561. And from the sixteenth century onwards French, British, Italian, Dutch and many other nationalities visited, providing a picture of how Bahrainis lived and worked.

Early rulers of Bahrain included Bimum, who governed the island about 1,800 bc, and Uperi, a contemporary of Argon 'the Assyrian'. Protected by a sea around it, Bahrain has had a continuous line of rulers from the beginning of the second millenium BC, about 4,000 years ago. The seventeenth and eighteenth centuries saw Bahrain occupied by various rulers, including Omanis and Persians. The Portuguese tried an unsuccessful comeback and even the Turks laid envious eyes on the island, but with disastrous results: their commander in the Gulf, Piri Rais, lost a number of treasure-laden ships off the north of Bahrain and this cost him his head.

The story of modern Bahrain begins in 1782 when Sheikh Ahmed al-Fatih, forebear of the Ruler Sheikh Isa, landed in Bahrain after his father had successfully repelled an attack on the Khalifa city of Zubara, on the Qatar peninsula. Ever since, the history of Bahrain has been linked with the Al-Khalifa dynasty.

A state like Bahrain has had its share of both heroes and villains and its history as a settled land is explained by its natural riches: fresh water, pearls, its agriculture and its central position astride one of the world's traditional trade routes. The association of Bahrain with Dilmun, legendary land of Gilgamesh, is well known: Gilgamesh came to Dilmun seeking the flower of everlasting life. Dilmun was the home of Ziusudra, sole survivor of the Flood, who had become immortal after his survival from the rising waters. Legends apart, Dilmun was a very real place and, like Bahrain, depended greatly on trade. Its merchants dealt in many goods, among the most important of which were copper and diorite, probably brought from Oman, and gold and ivory from India.

The names of some of these early Bahrain merchants survive, with some of their correspondence. There is in existence a letter sent to a trader, named Nanni, in which the writer complains: 'When you came you said, "I will give good ingots to Gimil-Sin". That is what you said, but you have not done so; you offered bad ingots to my messenger, saying "Take it or leave it". Who am I that you should treat me so contemptuously? Who is there among the Dilmun traders who has acted against me in this way?' *Plus ca change* . . . the complaining tone of one trader to another in commerce down through the ages.

CHAPTER NINE

Bahrain, I was to find, was still a largely traditional community where, with notable exceptions, women took a backseat. But this was quickly to change. When I arrived, most of the pre-marriage girls wore the abba, a black all-enveloping shift that covered them from head to toe, though leaving the face exposed. Two years later, the abba-wearing girls were almost in a minority as western fashions found a ready market among this emerging new generation. Hot pants were the rage among western wives, worn mostly discreetly and privately but this was very much several steps too far for young local girls. However, the ridiculous-looking platform shoes, with multi-coloured soles, were in vogue in Europe and were popular with local youths, who could be seen teetering and wobbling along the streets in Manama, drawing disapproving glances from puzzled locals.

The mosques were everywhere, with their elegant minarets from which the call to prayer would sound at intervals throughout the day. It was an island of contrasts, from the staggering wealth amassed by the merchant elite, dealing in everything from cars to cranes to air-conditioners, representing the world's leading insurance houses, and running a variety of travel agencies selling air tickets where the sky really was the limit, down to im- poverished families living in little more than 'barasti' shacks built from palm fronds on the edges of villages.

But no one starved and education and opportunity were there for everyone. Yet such poverty was a breeding ground for resent- ment, particularly among the Shias, who greatly outnumbered the Sunnis on the island; but the Sunnis were the ruling class. Sunnis are orthodox Muslims; Shias believe that after the death of the Prophet Mohamed his nephew and son-in-law, Ali, should have become the first Caliph. During the month of Muharram, Shias worldwide mark the martyrdom of Hasan and Husain, sons of Ali and only surviving grandsons of the Prophet. Bitterness between the two sects lives on, with periodic flare-ups.

Charity is one of the pillars of Islam; waqf – the giving of alms – was a constant feature and rigorously controlled; compassion was another. It was not unusual for a man to marry his brother's widow, however old, thus taking her into his own family, guaranteeing dignity and comfort for the rest of her days. Generosity is part of Arab life; to refuse hospitality towards a visitor – even an enemy – is unthinkable; coffee would be prepared and a meal pressed on the caller. On one of my early explorations of the island of Muharraq, where I had been warned that small boys had been known to stone westerners (this, I later found, stemmed from the generosity of earlier visitors not being extended by those who followed), I came upon a group of old men sitting under the propped-up hull of a fishing dhow they were repairing. A brass coffee pot was going the rounds; small bowls on the ground contained dates and segments of orange; beckoning, they urged me to sit with them. They wanted to know who I was, where I was going, what did I want on Muharraq; mentioning the names of locals I knew was enough introduction and we departed firm friends, an episode I look back on with fondness, to an age that then seemed timeless.

That same courtesy and impeccable manners were experienced by my wife in the suq, with constant offers of cold Pepsi and tiny thin-waisted glasses of black sweet tea. Nothing was too much trouble for her favourite dressmaker, even if she did catch sight of an eye gazing through a slit in the curtains as she undressed to try on her latest order. The suq was an endless fascination, with each street having its distinctive aroma: the pungency of the multi-coloured piles of spices heaped in boxes outside the shops; the musty smell of the Persian carpet shop where scores of large carpets were stacked, neatly folded; to see one close to the bottom was a major operation for the tiny Iranian owner. Not to your liking? It would be laboriously refolded and neatly replaced; I never saw him sell a carpet, except the two he sold me. He would sit at the entrance smoking his hubble-bubble; no hurry.

Other parts of the suq were more down to earth: the sweet smell of the fruit and vegetable market was a contrast to the powerful odour of the meat market where, amid flies in the open air, cleavers thumped down and blades flashed at each of the stalls; at the fish market, the stench was overwhelming as the morning's catch was dealt with, an enormous hamour being split in front of you, weighed and dumped in your palm-frond bag. For beautiful fresh fish, or for the famous Bahrain giant prawns, it was a gauntlet of smells worth running. There were other even earthier aromas. The suq was still primitive and plumbing was basic. It was not unusual in those early days to step round a pool of raw sewage as it seeped from a broken pipe.

In Bahrain, the pearls that had played such a major part in the island's economy through history were still important, though the mighty fleet that had put out to sea each year at the start of the diving season was gone. But pearl merchants still held large stocks. Bahraini pearls were once the wonder of the world and to view a gleaming pile displayed on the traditional red baize at dealers such as the Al-Mudaifa brothers, in the suq, is to see the real thing. They have lost none of their allure. As times changed, people changed with them; one of the prominent pearl merchants was absent for six months of the year, staying at his luxury apartment in London's West End and arriving to a VIP reception when he gambled nightly at the Playboy club.

Also in the suq I found the money changers, and the silversmiths and the gold merchants who sold baubles, bangles and worry beads made up of semi-precious stones. Each piece of precious metal was sold by weight; there was a margin for negotiation, but it was small. The price of gold ruled the suq – in the Gulf it was part of life. Every wife had an armful.

On the edge of the suq were the blacksmiths, standing in pits beside their anvils as they swung long-handled hammers, squashing the tiny sections of glowing red-hot rod until the heads mushroomed, to create sturdy bolts for the dhow builders; the smiths, glistening as the sweat ran down their bare chests, were as black as the heaps of charcoal that were piled next to the forges.

Nearby, on the coast, were the dhow yards. I would watch the teak planks from India being rough hewn with adzes, the sharp blades thudding down barely an inch from a bare foot. Complete, the dhow – the generic name is western but there are a myriad types – was a work of art. Building could take up to six months, the ribs propped up on the shore with poles. The cost for an oceangoing boat was £3,000; the British diesel engine to propel it through the Gulf waters could cost up to £10,000 – sails were now largely a thing of the past, though the sight of a far-off lateen sail filled by the wind, against azure water and a cloudless blue sky, was breathtakingly beautiful.

Why £10,000 for an engine? These were for the dhows engaged in the shadowy business of gold smuggling. The ten-tola bars, each the size of two tiny squares of chocolate, when smuggled into India brought an unbelievable profit. There were gold-smuggling syndicates throughout the Gulf. It was a high-risk operation, and complex. Each time the Indian authorities introduced faster patrol craft, the dhow engines were upgraded; patrol boats were never able to outrun a smugglers' dhow powered by its Rolls-Royce engine: the only thing that could was a naval four-inch shell, pitched 100 yards away. Even the bravest of nakhodas – dhow skippers – would then be persuaded to heave to.

But the voyages were usually uneventful; the illicit cargoes would be landed on the Indian coast and the glittering mini-ingots poured into baskets of dates; these would be fed to the camels that made up the baggage train before being led off into the mountains, past the government checkpoints. Once safely through, the bars would reappear as nature took its course.

Each week, as I explored deeper into the suq, the traders got to know me: the merchant who sold beautiful Arab robes, gold edged cloaks, intricately embroidered thobes; the clock repairer; the sandal shop, whose decorated flat-soled gaudy leather footwear from Saudi Arabia was worn by almost every Bahraini. Today, the sandal fashion has changed; gone is the colour, and the style is now plain and dull. Yet the suq still flourishes, its variety unchanging.

A humble beginning was no barrier to progress and the suq was full of prosperous self-made men, for the Bahrainis are a clever people with trade in their blood. One of the capital's many characters was Hassan Tarrada, who was brought up in a barasti – a palm-frond hut – near the historic twin minarets of the ruined mosque at the Suq-Al-Khamis, the Thursday market. As a boy he joined Bapco, staying there 30 years before opening his own store in the suq, selling safety equipment and also working for the government as an adviser six days a week.

If ever there was a success story about a local boy made good, it was Hassan. He provided me with an eye-witness account of the raid on the refinery by bombers of the Italian air force in late 1940. The flight by the four overloaded and obsolete aircraft was an epic, taking off from the Dodecanese islands in the Eastern Mediterranean, crossing the mountains of Lebanon and then following a course over the featureless desert, from Syria down the length of Saudi Arabia, to arrive over Bahrain before then finally making course for Eritrea, 3,000 miles in all. The bombers, each with a ton of small fragmentation bombs, were weighed down with fuel and flying at the very limit of their endurance. There was no margin for error.

But with the benefit of a tail wind, nine hours later they banked to roar over the northern tip of Bahrain. As they began their bombing run to the refinery, all lit up like a miniature Manhattan, it was the culmination of a masterpiece of planning. The bombs began to tumble out . . . and missed. The Italians had aimed for the gas flares a short distance from the main refinery, and the deadly cargo exploded harmlessly in the desert, and in one case next to a pile of coal.

Hassan, working the graveyard shift at the refinery, heard the explosions. 'I was scared and looked round for somewhere to hide,' he told me. He ran across to a large naphtha tank, a highly explosive product, and curled up underneath it. I said something about jumping out of the frying pan into the fire. 'It was a stout tank,' he protested.

He lived to see another day – and so did the bomber crews. They flew on to the Red Sea coast and then started the last leg, across to Eritrea 200 miles away, seized in the dictator Mussolini's war with the Ethiopia of the Emperor Haile Selassie, then known as Abyssinia. Each of the aircraft, powered by three Alfa-Romeo engines, landed with just 40 gallons of fuel. Italy claimed a great victory and the bomber crews made their way back home to a heroes' welcome.

The island was also known for its exuberant characters, wealthy Arabs from outside Bahrain who could become tired and emotional. Fists had been known to fly among these as arguments became heated. One of the smaller local hotels would then become like a scene from a Wild West film, the English manager told me, with chairs flying amid the crash of breaking glass. After one of these bouts of fisticuffs one of the protagonists, who received a black eye, decided he had been grievously wronged and set off in his American limousine to take his complaint to the very top – at 3am. He arrived at the palace of the Ruler still highly indignant and told the startled sentry that he insisted on a personal audience. Sheikh Isa eventually appeared, distinctly not amused at being disturbed. He heard the man out, noted his appearance, and the black eye, and then delivered a crushing one-liner: 'Stick to Pepsi-Cola next time.'

The Ruler has a mischievous sense of humour, and this was

demonstrated when Christine's car ran out of fuel on the desert road back from the beach at Zallaq, on the north-west of the island, with our two daughters in the back. As Sheikh Isa's Mercedes swished past, he noted the white Volkswagen Beetle at a standstill and told his driver to stop. He asked what was the problem. She told him, and he despatched a second car back to a filling station a mile and a half away. As the jerrycan of fuel was handed over, he told her, gravely but with a twinkle in his eye 'Running out of petrol in Bahrain? You should be ashamed of yourself.'

Personalities on the island ranged from the endearing to the downright eccentric, and this latter category definitely included one Sheikh Rashid, an elderly judge in the local court who had decided to become a Scotsman by adoption. He acquired full Highland dress, from kilt to sporran to stockings, wore it on official expatriate occasions, and delighted in being addressed as 'Sheikh McRashid'. He became a friend and, confessing to periodic indifferent health, told me his secret. 'I don't need a local doctor,' he confided. 'I have my own special physician: Dr Haig,' and he would raise a glass of a famous branded scotch. As a judge he could be forthright, and woe betide anyone who did not accord him what he thought was proper respect. One evening he recounted to me details of a case that morning. When a man was brought before him accused of theft, he stopped the local prosecutor in mid-sentence. 'I don't want to hear any evidence,' he said. 'I can see from his face that he's guilty. Six months.' I told this story to a police officer friend. 'If only all our cases could be as easy,' he sighed.

The Bahrainis generally had a great sense of humour, and liked nothing more than a good chuckle. The ruler's majlis was in many ways a public forum and those who regularly attended it knew each other well. The story – perhaps apocryphal – was still being told, with much hilarity, of a well-known merchant at the majlis of a previous ruler, who suddenly let out a loud fart. The ruler, startled, looked up and everyone's gaze swivelled round to the hapless man. His response was quick under the circumstances. 'You come to this majlis, give out your money, and keep your wind,' he pronounced loftily. 'I come here, lose my wind and keep my money.' It was almost an echo of an incident at the court of the Queen in Elizabethan England recorded by the diarist John Aubrey. This time the culprit was a distinguished earl, who was so overcome with embarrassment that he went into exile for some years. On his return, he presented himself at the court again. 'Welcome back, my lord,' the Virgin Queen called out on espying him. 'We have quite forgot the fart.'

There was one special Bahraini, my great friend Jassim Al-Ameer, grandson of a distinguished Saudi brought across to oversee Manama, whose refreshing frankness and honesty brightened many a day for me. Jassim, who worked for the aluminium smelter's personnel department, was among that rare breed, a man with no bias whose counsel was to save me from many unintended faux pas. As a newcomer, I had already picked up several local habits, among them a great slowness in coming to the point, approaching a sensitive subject from many directions before gently and finally touching upon it.

'Mr Trimbee,' he told me sternly, 'this is not my way. You are wriggling around like this,' and he made a gesture like a fish swimming in the water. 'I go direct,' and he rammed his arm forward, like a spear. Chastened, I had to agree. But on other things, sometimes I did know best. Jassim became the proud owner of a very large and gleaming second-hand Mercedes. 'Your insurance must be through the roof,' I commented. 'I don't bother with things like that,' he said. 'I just go for the barest minimum.' 'A big mistake,' I counselled. He shrugged. But some weeks later, he came to see me. 'Mr Trimbee, you were right. My wife wrapped the Mercedes round a lamppost. It's a write-off. I've lost all that money. And I can't afford another.'

If ever there was a case of inshallah, this was one. But

unabashed, he finally managed to buy a tiny Japanese car on hire purchase, and it was proudly displayed outside his house in the brand new Isa Town development, as I arrived for one of the many barbecues we enjoyed with him, as his many children played.

His father imported Persian carpets, and on one visit to my home Jassim was shocked to see a stuffed mongoose in the act of killing a stuffed cobra, displayed in the living room. I told him it was a present from a Bahraini friend, just back from a trip to Bombay. 'You must throw it out immediately. My father had one, it was full of bugs. They ate all his Persian carpets.' He paused for effect. 'And, Mr Trimbee, ate them very nicely.' Mongoose and cobra went straight in the refuse bin.

In this hot-house of unbridled commerce, with fortunes to be made for local traders, there could be temptations for westerners, and some did succumb. A young Bahraini businessman later turned politician told me of one incident involving a middle-ranking RAF officer. The air force was carrying out extension work at its Muharraq headquarters and was reclaiming an area of land from the sea. A contractor had been hired to haul in and dump hundreds of tons of desert sand, to build up foundations. Keeping tally of the loads was the officer, watching with a clipboard and pen. My Bahraini friend, who was working with the contrtactor, was told to befriend him and he duly did, taking him and his family out to dinner frequently at local hotels.

One day, after fifteen loads were delivered by truck, the foolish officer was handed the delivery note to sign. But the note was for twenty loads. He hesitated, then signed it. The next day, a present of a hi-fi set arrived at the officer's home. The pattern continued, but the discrepancies grew wider and wider, each time signed off by the officer. By the time the project was complete and all the distorted invoices were paid, the loads of infill paid for were thirty per cent more than they actually were, bringing a windfall for the contractor – and serious trouble for the officer when the glaring difference was uncovered by a routine audit. For bribes that were paltry by any standards, he had sacrificed his career. 'That poor man was recalled to England and brought in front of a court martial,' said the young Bahraini, full of contrition. 'I heard that he served a prison sentence.'

There was one people whose value to Bahrain cannot be underestimated. Palestinians played an important part in island life. As a dispossessed people, they were scattered across the world, never able to go home because their home was lost to them, in a tragic, ironic echo of the diaspora of the tribes of Israel many centuries before. They were multi-talented and looked to the Gulf states for sanctuary, where they were to prove indispensable to rulers in a variety of roles until, after years, citizenship would become reality. Where once they had looked out over citrus trees, now they looked out over desert, but were grateful for this Arab brotherhood based on a shared blood and the caring tradition of Islam. For too many years they lived like strangers in a foreign land, always feeling they were on the outside, looking in, until at last they felt themselves finally absorbed into their adopted homeland. Bahrain was to benefit hugely from the expertise and qualifications of these newcomers. Palestine was to provide head teachers, lawyers, accountants and a range of other professions which the island had yet to develop.

Prominent in Bahrain was Ahmed Suleiman, mainstay of the island's broadcasting service, which he joined in 1965 from the BBC Arabic service in London. His voice, heavy, low and instantly recognisable, could be heard giving the commentary at most major official functions in Bahrain. Short and bulky, he was a familiar figure at the microphone and would travel abroad with the Ruler on official visits, sending back recorded commentaries. He established Bahrain's English service in 1976, as the head of Radio Bahrain. One evening, when I was a guest at his home in Manama, his wife began to talk wistfully of the family's orange groves left behind in Palestine. He cut her short. 'Don't even think of them,' he said brusquely. 'They're gone, gone for ever. We must look only to the future, our future here.' It was a poignant and sad moment Ahmed, broadcaster extraordinary, who had also been a freelance in Bahrain for the Reuters news agency, based in Fleet Street, London, died in his adopted home in 2005, aged seventy-six, and was to be greatly missed.

Another well-known Palestinian was Adnan Bseisu, who came to Bahrain from Gaza in 1966 to become manager of the Arab Bank. Then followed a distinguished career. He joined Gulf Aviation, as it then was, as finance manager, moving to the newly-founded Arab Latin-American Bank as deputy chief. Public-spirited and a prominent and long-serving Rotarian, he played a leading role in the life of Bahrain.

On a visit to Dubai I met Isa Shoman, Palestinian head of the Arab Bank there, a larger-than-life and heavily overweight jovial figure. We met at a social evening and found we shared a common interest: Havana cigars. 'They're my passion,' he enthused. 'Come to my office tomorrow at 10am and we shall smoke one.' I duly turned up, and he was waiting with a cup of coffee and a new, unopened box of enormous Montecristos, the biggest in the range. Wielding a long steel cutter, he deftly removed the end of one of these monsters and handed it to me. We sat chatting, puffing away and producing clouds of smoke. As he beamed at me, I began to realise that I was feeling distinctly queasy. Cigars are all very well, but there is a time and place for them, and I slowly realised that this was not 10 o'clock in the morning. Waves of nausea began to sweep over me and I eventually managed to get to my feet, pleading another pressing appointment. Breezily, he closed up the box and handed it to me, together with the cutter. 'My present,' he said. I staggered outside into the hot sun, knees almost buckling and head spinning. Every time I use that cigar cutter, it brings back memories. Isa was a true Palestinian, warm, welcoming, and generous to a fault.

The population was cosmopolitan, and it was always a surprise to westerners to find that living in Manama was a small Jewish community, a testimony to the state's well-known tolerance to other faiths. This community, once thriving, dates back to the 1880s when Iraqi Jewish traders first settled. They became part of mercantile life, trading with their former home and as they modestly thrived, so their numbers expanded, eventually totalling more than a thousand. There was a Hebrew school, and even a synagogue.

But today the synagogue, a single-storey building in one of the maze of tiny streets that make up old Manama, is unused, with the benches in the prayer hall piled up against a wall. It was built in the 1930s and once in regular use. But in the wake of the creation of the state of Israel in 1948, when riots broke out in Bahrain, Jewish homes were looted and a Jewish woman died, most of Bahrain's Jews left for Britain or the United States. A smaller number opted to go to Israel, a decision they later regretted; they found their new life there did not compare with the one they had left behind.

During the riots the synagogue was sacked and the sacred Torah scrolls vanished. A lifetime later, they were returned to one of the leading members of the Jewish community. The stranger who handed them over reportedly said his family had suffered bereavement and sickness ever since, and he felt he had to restore them to their rightful owners.

Perfume, fabrics and foreign exchange. These were sectors where the bustling newcomers had thrived. Over the years they integrated well, joining Bahraini merchants in joint ventures and playing a role in the local Rotary organisation. As Rouben Rouben, in the electronics business, explained in 2008: 'We consider ourselves Bahrainis. My religion is Jewish and Bahrain is my home.'

Apart from the 1948 riots, and similar disturbances that followed the Six-Day War, Bahrain's Jews never experienced prejudice. There was one ugly incident in the early 1970s, during Ramadhan. As the field gun in Manama was fired to mark sundown and the traditional breaking of the fast, the suq emptied as people sped home to eat. One Jewish trader remained in his narrow-fronted shop where he dealt in currency. No one saw the intruder who stealthily entered, and no one heard the pistol shot that killed his victim. It was more than an hour before the body was found; the shop had been ransacked and hundreds of Bahraini dinars taken. Gun crime was unknown in Bahrain. A widespread search by police failed to reveal any clues. The murder was never solved.

Other Jews from the Gulf area took a high profile far away. A branch of the Khedouri family moved to Hong Kong via Bombay and Shanghai, founding the power company that now supplies electricity to seventy-five per cent of the people. Michael Kadoorie harvested a clutch of honours as a renowned philanthropist, including a knighthood from the Queen in 2005. In the United States, Ezra Zilkha is today one of the 400 richest Americans, after a journey that took a lifetime, from Baghdad to Manhattan, where he became a leading banker.

Bahrain's Jews were always low profile and widely respected by their fellow merchants. Members played their part in public life. Abraham Nonoo in 1934 was elected to Manama Municipality, the first elected municipal body. Then in 2002 his grandson, also Abraham, joined the Shura council, the parliament's upper house, appointed by King Hamed. Four years later Houda Ezra Nonoo joined the same council. Then in 2006 she was named by the King as the state's ambassador to the United States, the first Jewish ambassador of any Arab country.

But by 2009 the Jewish community in Bahrain had shrunk to around 36. The continued existence of the synagogue is due to the wishes of the King himself; after it fell into disuse. The community offered it to the state; the King insisted that it remain a synagogue.

CHAPTER TEN

As the weeks wore on, the work of producing each edition fell into a pattern. One morning was earmarked for my 'calls', enjoyable hours spent visiting my many contacts, taking coffee with them and gleaning whatever I could for the next issue. Rarely did that time fail to bear fruit. But one day I reaped a bumper harvest.

The personnel manager of an oil-drilling company, Offshore Venezuela, had struck an informal deal with me that, in return for the paper carrying small pieces on his operation's 'lost-time hours' – accident statistics of no interest to anyone but his employees and insurance company – he would supply me with any snippets of news concerning his multi-national staff.

One morning I drew a blank. 'Nothing much happening,' said Ron Hemp, a burly, talkative East Anglian continually harassed by his American bosses. I got up to go. As I opened the door, he asked: 'Are you a soccer fan?' 'Not really,' I said. 'Have you ever heard of the Robledo brothers?' 'Can't say I have.' The brothers, once famous in England, had played in the winning team in a British Cup Final. One of them, Eduardo, worked for Offshore. 'What about him?' I asked. 'Well, he's vanished.'

That was how I landed the paper's first – and probably greatest – exclusive. The missing man, once famous to Geordie fans as Ted Robledo, played for Newcastle United and with his brother George was in the Cup Final of 1952. George scored the only goal, a header, to beat Arsenal. His playing days over, Ted returned home to Chile, and then came out to the Gulf to work on an oil rig.

He was ashore in Dubai on leave when he met up with the German skipper of a coastal tanker and decided to spend a few days leisurely steaming down the coast. He was never seen again. A phone call to Dubai fleshed out the story. The thirty-year-old skipper, Heinz Bessenich, had been arrested and accused of 'wilfully and unlawfully causing death in a brutal and savage manner . . .'

I kept all details secret until publication day, when our front page banner headline shouted: Ex-soccer star vanishes in Gulf. A subsidiary line added: Tanker skipper accused. The story carried the tag: Mirror Exclusive. Days later Bahrain's Foreign Minister, Sheikh Mohammed bin Mubarak, told me: 'I read the paper in London. The "exclusive" line made me feel so proud.'

The story burst like a small bomb among the western media. Their troubleshooters were on the next plane out to Dubai; hotel rooms, already limited, became at a premium. The news desks of a dozen leading newspapers not only in Britain but across Europe kept my phone permanently engaged.

I flew down to Dubai to interview the sheikhdom's chief of police, Jack Briggs, a tiny bundle of energy. Briggs, from Blackpool, had made a career of police work in the Gulf, serving in Qatar then moving further south to become the trusted security aide to Dubai's Ruler, Sheikh Rashid Al-Makhtoum. He was fluent in Arabic, having taken a degree course in Britain in addition to fitting in his work policing the bustling dynamic state. Sitting in his tiny office in the old police fort, barely changed in 50 years, he told me what he could. Robledo, it was believed, had embarked on a drinking session with the well-built Bessenich. This, said Briggs, was believed to have got out of hand; he was killed and it was thought that the German skipper had thrown him overboard. That was the police case. The body was never found.

The case wore on, with Bessenich in custody, having returned voluntarily from Athens and being awarded legal aid. The court asked that 'special care be taken for his comfort' while on remand. The trial date was fixed for a month later; the maximum sentence was life imprisonment. It was the first time in more than ten years that a European had appeared before a British court in the Gulf on a murder charge.

Bessenich throughout protested his innocence. Speaking in good English, he insisted that the disappearance of Robledo was 'just a tragic happening'. At a preliminary hearing, the court was told that the skipper had made no report of a missing passenger. The skipper's Indian steward testified that Bessenich had told him, on the return leg from Muscat to Dubai: 'If anybody asks, you are to say there were no passengers.' He had earlier seen two knives hanging in Bessenich's cabin. A day later, he noticed that only one was there.

Bessenich was employed by the Delmon Navigation Company, a subsidiary of Gray Mackenzie. He complained later that his bosses, displaying a fine sense of British impartiality, had sacked him five days before his first court appearance. At the trial a British judge, bewigged and gowned despite the heat outside, sat with three independent assessors, a French woman and two men, one German and one Briton, drawn from Dubai's community. The prosecution at 'Her Britannic Majesty's Court of the Trucial State of Dubai' claimed that the skipper had told a 'web of lies'. His actions in not reporting Robledo's absence, in not turning the ship round to mount a search, in not sending out a radio alert, in denying that Robledo had been on the ship, and in destroying all material evidence of Robledo's presence, were because he had killed him, the prosecution said.

The missing man's brother, Walter, sat in the courtroom as the inevitable verdict was announced: not guilty. The judge said that while he had not been impressed by Bessenich's defence of his actions, there was insufficient evidence.

The blond skipper, from Porzwahn, who never once lost his composure during his two and a half months behind bars, walked out into the sun a free man. The mystery was never solved. But there was a strange postscript: some years later, in Dubai, I met the British police officer who had been tasked in putting together the prosecution's case. Each time they thought they had a break-through, he said, the evidence collapsed. Then they found a blood-stained sheet from the skipper's cabin. He told them that his girlfriend had been a virgin and it was the result of their first night together. The girl was traced to Bahrain; police flew up to interview her. Yes, she said, his story was true.

Bessenich flew to Beirut and then to Europe, to the girl he had become engaged to just before his arrest. And then, just like Robledo, he vanished.

Formal occasions were a regular feature of life in Bahrain, and as editor of the local English-language paper I was invited to most. That meant black tie, and frantic minutes spent struggling with a bow tie in front of the mirror, trying desperately to remember the instructions from bow-tie-wearing friends. Then it was off to the palace at Rifa'a for the reception in honour of whatever high-ranking dignitary happened to be visiting.

The car park would be crowded, as usual, and I would join the throng of guests in dinner jackets, white or black, and Bahrainis in their formal gold-edged robes, immaculate headdresses and white thobes. The Ruler would stand at the entrance, flanked by armed Bedu guards and with the VIP beside him, as he welcomed each arrival, addressing everyone by name, even though some of the Europeans he could have met only once or twice. That was a remarkable quality of Sheikh Isa – although partially blind in one eye, he had what seemed a totally retentive memory for faces. He never forgot. He was known for his ability, on returning from a visit outside Bahrain, to notice who had been absent from the large crowd gathered at the airport to welcome him home. Any of the usual visitors to his daily majlis at the palace who might be absent for a couple of days, without explanation, could expect to be asked, with that Arab courtesy that the Ruler had a special gift for, why he had not been seen.

He had a way of dealing with troublemakers. A writer on one of the Arabic publications would pen particularly waspish comments.

After a run of these, the man would be summoned to the palace. His health would be anxiously inquired after; did he have any worries? 'You are our son,' he would be assured, 'your happiness is important to us.' Perhaps an envelope of dinars would be discreetly passed over. The parting would be accompanied by protestations of undying loyalty. As the pinprick articles continued, this routine would be repeated over a period of months. Then, literally, bang. The bang of a cell door closing. A period of reflection would follow. The wayward son would emerge apparently penitent, make his appearance the next day at the palace, and again exchange pledges of love and fealty, probably pleading momentary impoverishment for which there would be speedy relief. Honour was satisfied, until the next time.

For troublemakers of a darker hue, there could be prison sentences on the bare, craggy island of Jidda, off Bahrain's northwestern tip, complete with English warder, a veteran of prisons east of Suez who spent two-week stints on the island before being ferried back to civilisation on the main island. The Englishman, held in great affection by his charges, would spend his free weekends getting drunk at the British Club. After the return trip to Jidda, his dhow would be met by two prisoners with a wheelbarrow and he would be trundled home to his quarters.

He was a big man in every way. One of the many political detainees told me years later how his jailer would always stroll up the corridors with a huge key ring that jangled noisily. 'Can't you be quieter?' he was asked. 'I do this deliberately,' he said. 'I don't want to know what you bastards get up to (there were strict rules) and I like to give advance warning so that you can hide away whatever I'm not supposed to see.'

The same ex-prisoner described to me a mini-mutiny by some troublesome inmates. While out of their cells for a period of exercise, they jumped their warder. The next moment the broad-shouldered Englishman was rolling on the ground, under a kicking, punching, screaming crowd. With an effort, he threw them off. 'This is not fair,' he roared. 'One at a time, one at a time.' The assailants, possessed of that innate Bahraini sense of fair play, then queued to take their turn in being felled by his ham-like fists. Honour was satisfied, order was restored; the matter was never mentioned to the warder's superiors back at Manama's police fort.

The Ruler, though diminutive, was a lion-hearted man who stood up to the blustering of his menacing neighbour across the water, Iran, with resolve and defiance. When the rapprochement was finally sealed in 1971 the Shah, later to be deposed in a bloodless coup engineered by the West, sent his foreign minister to Bahrain to seal the new age of closer relations. The reception was larger and grander than usual, and with a difference. As the foreign minister arrived, dapper in black tie and wearing, I noticed, a pair of dark-blue and gold Gucci velvet slippers, a greatly strengthened palace guard of nearly a hundred goatee-bearded Bedu formed a huge crescent in the moonlit courtyard, each swathed in a double bandolier holding magazines for their Kalashnikovs, which they held by the barrel, the butt resting on the ground. Their black robes formed a sinister contrast to the bright clothing of the guests and the rich hues of the Persian carpets. The message was clear: we may be small, but we'd be more trouble than you'd imagine.

The palace banquets were brief. The guests would be ushered in, taking their place at the long tables – there was no precedence other than for the VIPs with the Ruler – and immediately would begin to demolish the mounds of steaming saffron rice, tearing great chunks off the roast sheep on huge oval dishes, stuffed with dates, nuts and hard-boiled eggs. Eating would last little more than ten minutes; a sweet would follow, perhaps a small dish of pink blancmange, then the coffee. Then as the Ruler rose to his feet, so would the guests, and after washing their rice-flecked hands in water poured by servants carrying large jugs, rinsing them in bowls of rose water, they would hurry out, pausing only to bid farewell to the Ruler and possibly help themselves to a couple of cigars from boxes held out by more servants. The banquet leftovers, always enough to feed a small army, would then be summarily despatched by sentries, drivers, servants and hangers-on. The cars would roar away to join a multi-coloured tailback on the dark road down to Manama. Most of the guests would then go on to have a second dinner at their own homes, to be consumed at greater leisure.

The formal dinners were carefully orchestrated, but there was at least one occasion when things did not quite go according to plan. Through a misunderstanding, perhaps a mistaken signal, the sentries, drivers and servants were let into the banqueting hall before the guests had gone in. The food was cleared in a matter of minutes in a frenzy of snatching, clawing, gnawing and gulping. One who was there told me how one guard thrust his arm deep into the rice, to have another opportunist guest opposite seize it and sink his teeth in it. The real guests, still outside in the courtyard, were treated to a bizarre silhouette show through the windows as dark figures leapt on the tables, arms flying as the food was scattered in this unexpected banqueting bonanza.

My working week would begin on Monday, after my one very brief day off. I would arrive in the office at 8am tired and hungover from the previous night's cocktail parties, usually multiple, attendance at which was essential for tuning in to the state's gossip and learning of latest developments. Stories garnered would range from anything for the paper's gossip column to news of big deals and political to-ings and fro-ings.

As I sipped my first coffee of the day I would liaise with my secretary, Beryl, and deal with the inevitable flow of grumbles, queries and calls that any editor has to live with, fending off some and dealing diplomatically with others. After dealing with correspondence and routine admin, from paying the cleaners and messengers to accepting yet more cocktail party dates and invitations to dinner, I would then make a start on editorial work for the coming issues: designing and sub-editing feature pages and regular features like the horoscope column, highly popular with expatriates and Arabs alike and which was supplied from an agency in London literally weeks in advance. In between all this I would snatch phone conversations, collecting stories, confirming gossip, setting up interviews, scribbling down notes all the time. You never stopped. This was essentially a one-man editorial business. You are fighting the clock. In a spare moment from the hectic pace of laying the ground, I would try to get on with writing a story.

With the approach of lunchtime, around 11.30, I would leave the office to drop in on anything up to half a dozen contacts, say ten to fifteen minutes with each and the obligatory cup of coffee; more gossip, more 'touching base'. The countless calls were also a wonderful way of promoting the paper, a one-man PR exercise. On Sundays – my day off – there was the chore of attending the Rotary Club lunch which, while again a good PR exercise, rarely seemed to yield anything special for the paper. The bulk of the stories related to the westerners living in the tiny state, but there was nonetheless a constant flow of stories from the locals them-selves who, as they learnt to trust the newspaper, would tip off the editor, using their inside knowledge.

For lunch I would return home, for a brief period of normality and sanity and, in summer, take a two-hour siesta, with the temperature outside sometimes 110 degrees, sleeping the sleep of the dead until 4pm, then staggering from the bed like Lazarus raised, splashing water on my face and returning to the office. There, dragging out my notebook and various pieces of paper, backs of envelopes and scraps, I would quickly – through practice – rattle out the many stories gleaned from interviews for the women's page and business page. That done, I would list the pictures needed for Beryl to book with our brilliant photographer Abdulla Khan, design more news pages, edit the copy and make one of the countless treks through the dusty streets to the little printing house, handing the bundle of papers to the ever-smiling and ever-patient Matthew who could never get used to the constant flow of Anglo-Saxon epithets which always seem to accompany the production of an English-language paper. He once said to me in indignation: 'Mr Trimbee, I am not a bugger!'

Then it would be home again for a shower and change, and out with Christine for the first of up to three cocktail parties, before almost invariably going on to a dinner party. Home again, perhaps at midnight, and I would collapse exhausted into bed. The price for running a Gulf newspaper was high.

As the list of our many local contributors expanded, we discovered the occasional gem. One such was Duncan Gilchrist, who worked at the Bapco refinery, who called in one day and hesitatingly offered some of his poetry for publication. Duncan, looking like a rocker, all hipster jeans and studded black belt, proved a gifted poet and we carried several of his works, illustrated with line drawings. One of his more whimsical offerings, about the island's earth station, which provided phone links with the outside world, began:

> Bahrain's earshell, poised, precise,
> Catching trembling waves of urgent need . . .

and ended:

> Happy birthday, Mother dear,
> Please send a hundred pounds.

There was a poet of a different hue, a Bahraini, who strode dishevelled into the office to book advertising space for intended dhow trips, offering Arab music and typical Arab meals, all in blank verse. We ran these advertisements for some weeks, and received several requests for further information. Eventually Ebrahim Eshaq questioned why we were carrying them. 'I think he may be slightly eccentric,' I offered by way of explanation. 'No, he's mad,' said

Eshaq emphatically. 'Don't accept any more advertisements from him.' In the event, he never paid a single dinar.

In many ways, Bahrain was a magical place, with a history reaching back thousands of years. Our home was surrounded by prehistoric burial grounds and in our area, Jufair, I always sensed an atmosphere, an almost eerie sensation which I also felt in the house itself. From the moment we moved in I somehow knew – and I have never considered myself psychic – that there was a presence there, and I instinctively knew that this was of a woman. One night, when my family was back in England on holiday, I awoke at 3am with the feeling of being suffocated.

Still half asleep, I tried to move, but couldn't. Something seemed to be sitting on my chest and in my barely conscious state I sensed it was a little old woman, dressed in black – and she was trying to strangle me. I fought and thrashed around and began to realise that whatever this spectre was, I was the stronger. With a final effort, I threw off what I thought had been pinioning me down, broke loose and sat up on the edge of the bed, gasping for breath. As I tried to pull myself together, I said loudly in the darkened room, 'Go away and don't come back, you old bitch'. I climbed back into bed and went straight off to sleep. The spell, if spell there was, had been broken. I was never troubled again.

And there could be other night visitors. I awoke early one morning, the family now back, feeling something heavy on top of me; as I moved, it slid down to my waist. My God, a rat on the bed! I leapt up, jerked on the light and as Christine struggled into fearful wakefulness, began a frantic search under the bed. Nothing. The night visitor came again a week later. And it was only after another fortnight that I discovered the culprit. I had developed the habit of going off to sleep on my back, with an arm wrapped around my neck. After some hours, the blood flow would be cut off, the arm would become numb, and when I moved it would fall down on my body without any sensation, an explanation that Christine was greatly relieved to hear.

But these false alarms proved a forerunner to the real thing. Christine went up to bed one evening, threw back the covers . . . and out jumped a seriously larger-than-life bewhiskered rat which fled up the stairs leading to the flat roof. This particular rat had scaled the side of our house by finding a grip on the rough concrete screed with which the breeze-block walls had been sprayed, and the door at the top had been left open to secure a slight night-time breeze. A rat-catcher duly appeared and set his trap, which took only 24 hours to prove deadly effective.

What proved more difficult to conquer were our other nocturnal visitors. Like many houses in Bahrain, ours was virtually overrun by cockroaches. These loathsome, industrial-size creepy-crawlies were a fact of life and constant spraying was essential, though of limited effect. As dusk fell, they became bold. It was quite usual for me, having gone to bed with a glass of water within reach, to wake in the morning to find a drowned cockroach in it. This was a problem that just had to be lived with and I eventually accepted their presence, living in a state of siege, only declaring all-out war if one actually ran up my naked back as I lay in bed, sweating gently through the long hot summer nights.

When I went on leave, the cockroaches would take over, until I discovered my secret weapon. I found a German product to be highly effective and before going away would sprinkle a pile of the russet-brown powder in each of our three bathrooms, near the drainage grates in the floor. On my return I would gingerly push open the bathroom doors to hear a rustling sound and be met with a strange, pungent smell. Dead cockroaches literally in their hundreds would be piled up on the inside of the doors. There were neighbours who claimed that cockroaches have no smell. I know better.

These disgusting light-brown lozenges, all legs and drooping antennae, could get anywhere. Once when I was having a bath, one appeared, feelers waving, through the overflow grill by the taps. And one morning, as my family sat down to breakfast, the familiar shape of a cockroach was seen high on the wall, squirming between the blades of an extractor fan. But for sheer chutzpah, there was the time when, as one of my children was about to eat her breakfast cereal, the cornflakes suddenly erupted in the bowl and up popped another. It was difficult to say who was the more surprised.

CHAPTER ELEVEN

Life was hectic: the grinding routine of producing a newspaper at a printing press barely equipped to do it was gradually reducing me to a state of exhaustion; and even though I had managed to stabilise the process to a point when I would finally walk out of the press at around 4am most Sundays, I would be up barely four hours later to arrive at the Ruler's palace in time to see him as he was driven up to the entrance in his gleaming black Mercedes-Benz 600 limousine.

That apart, the compensations were many, not least among them the Americans living in Bahrain, warm, welcoming, generous and unfailingly helpful to this Englishman producing a little news-paper and continually on the quest for stories. First among them, and the uncrowned king of Bahrain, was Jo Josephson, the president of Bapco, slim, grey-haired, steely-blue-eyed and husky voiced. He was to become a close friend. Jo, from Oregon, had come to Bahrain in the late 1940s, and stayed. To the Ruler, and to his brother, the highly-competent Prime Minister, Sheikh Khalifa, he was addressed affectionately as 'Ami' – uncle. Jo, in his late 50s, was an oilman to the core, but the years had rounded off rough edges and he was also a natural diplomat and politician. He was trusted implicitly by the Ruler, and with good reason.

After I had gained his confidence, no trouble was too much, and this message was passed down the sprawling Bapco corporation that was the main employer on the island and also a major presence. Bapco not only produced oil but also refined large quantities piped under the sea from Saudi Arabia, across a narrow strait, at its sprawling coastal refinery; dotted across Bahrain was a network of filling stations, each with the Bapco sign.

Once a week Jo would hold 'open house' at his large colonial-style residence, Al Bustan, in Manama, and a dozen miles from Awali, where he would welcome all comers with a drink. That was his contribution to the social scene; for the rest of the week he eschewed the constant round of cocktail parties as a waste of time, maintaining a discipline of going out only one or two evenings a week. The big-hearted Jo insisted on throwing a party at Al Bustan for Christine and myself. 'Invite who you like. Bring your swimming costumes – perhaps there'll be some skinny dipping.' Rounding up a crowd of friends was easy and a memorable evening followed, with Jo in fine form, complaining that the dry martinis – his speciality – were being made too weak and putting at ease those, and there were many, who were clearly slightly in awe of this iconic – in Bahrain – figure. It was the final seal of acceptance for us among the expatriate community, and we left, tired and pleasantly full of American steak, at 1am. There was, alas, no skinny dipping.

Some weeks later, Jo rang me. 'I've been invited to Beirut by Middle East Airlines to pick up some award. It'll be boring on my own. Want to come along?' Did I! The garden capital was then the Paris of the Middle East; I had grown accustomed to stories of its beauty, sophistication, and hustle-bustle life. We flew out first class, cosseted by the staff of MEA, undoubtedly one of the world's best airlines. Leaving the desert landscape behind us, two and a half hours later, after crossing snowy mountains, the 707 touched down at Beirut. The aircraft doors swung open and warm air wafted in, bringing with it the scent of jasmine. Lebanon, the biblical land of milk and honey.

Jo was put up in the five-star Hotel St George; ranking not quite so highly, I was ferried by Rolls-Royce to a more modest down-town establishment in a plunging street. Minutes later, I was in my room, making the most of an ice-cold Amstel beer and watching through the shutters as women opposite swept their balconies among the potted plants and gossiped. The first day was my intro-duction to a traditional Lebanese lunch: mezza. On the restaurant terrace in the warm May sunshine, Ziad Sablini, the airline's PR man, explained: 'It's usual to have a hundred of these small dishes, each different. We're having only about fifty. I must apologise.' Fifty proved well beyond my capacity to sample, with the delicious and better-known hommus, crushed-mint tabbouleh, eggplant, baba ghannoush, falafel, lamb kebabs and olives crowded out by a host of other delicacies.

The next two days I had pretty much to myself as Jo went out on his official business; Sablini laid on a series of trips: to Baalbeck, high in the mountains, in the Bekaa Valley later to become notorious as a stronghold of terrorists. The ancient city, with colonnaded courtyards, ruined temples but with Corinthian columns still standing proud, was a monument to the glory that once was Rome's. The visit was worth the hair-raising ride at speed, round hairpin bends, tyres squealing and horns blaring. The Lebanese had perfected the art of driving to within less than an inch of their life. Almost. Wrecks at every corner testified that some had learnt less well than others.

Another day took me to Byblos, further north on the coast and with a castle built by the Crusaders. Everywhere were the vivid blooms of flowers, and warm, damp newspaper packages of jasmine blooms were pressed into my hand by opportunistic little boys as the car waited at traffic lights; the entrepreneurial spirit of the Lebanese started young.

The evenings found the socialising in full swing, with Jo, fuelled by countless dry martinis that were eventually to his satisfaction, relating anecdote after anecdote. But the grand finale was to be the last night: a trip to the Casino du Liban, outside Beirut, where the fabled floor show lived up to its billing as the Greatest Show on Earth. In front of a packed audience of plump, well-dressed Lebanese and their sleek wives, or probably girlfriends, in the latest Paris creations, act followed spectacular act; then attendants made sure the crescent aisles running horizontally through the vast auditorium were clear. There were whoops, and war-painted

Red Indians brandishing tomahawks galloped through on pinto ponies; silence followed the initial gasps of surprise, and then elephants filed through, each trunk grasping the tail of the one ahead, swaying from side to side. I had to rub my eyes. Was this really happening? But it was not over. There was a rumble, and the steel-slatted aisle at my feet began to move; rattling, it was drawn away to vanish somewhere. Splashing followed as the space underneath filled with water. Then canoes began to appear, each carrying Indians in full war dress who paddled right through the audience in the very heart of Lebanon. Spectacular? Undoubtedly. Clearly no expense spared. Just a little decadent? Probably, but who cared.

However, for the audience, and for Jo, in tartan trousers and boot-string tie, who had sat tapping his fingers on his knees in boredom as the show unfolded, the real business of the night was about to begin. 'I'm going down to the tables,' he huskily told me. 'Coming?' Following his bustling figure beneath the chandeliers, we descended a floor to the gaming rooms. 'I need to change some money,' I faltered. 'I'll catch up with you in a minute.' This was the big time, I told myself, I'll just have to go with the flow. As the cashier flashed literally wads of high-denomination notes, dollars, sterling, you name it, I proffered £20 in Bahraini dinars. He gave me what could have been a slightly contemptuous look, and handed over tokens for the slot machines; I had no intention of playing roulette. The machines were clicking and whirring, literally in full spin as the Lebanese crowded around them, ladies grasping jewelled evening bags and the men large Havanas and sometimes their partners as well. Here goes. I strode up to a machine and fed in a token, and jerked the lever. Nothing. The equivalent of £2 gone. In went another; another £2 gone (was this fair to my wife? I wondered). I popped in another token, realising that I was just another loser. The fruit symbols flicked round and gradually each jerked to a stop, first one bar, then another, then . . . a third. There was a pause. Then the machine rumbled and from its belly crashed out a veritable mound of tokens. A hundred poundsworth. And remember, this was 1971 and my salary was only £60 a week; Britain had just gone over to decimal currency, but a pound was still a pound. I needed no persuasion to quit while I was most definitely ahead. Filling my trouser pockets, then my jacket pockets, and grasping the rest double-handedly, I bore them off, back to the same cashier who seemed if anything even less interested than before. My original stake, plus the winnings, safely back in my wallet, I set off in search of Jo.

We bumped into each other. 'How'd you get on, partner?' 'Great!' I gasped. 'I've just won a hundred quid.' 'A hundred pounds, what's that?' he shot back. 'I've just blown two thousand bucks.'

The Americans were an unobtrusive presence in Bahrain. There may have been momentous events, with the astronaut Alan Shepard playing golf on the Moon, and Nixon limbering up for his landslide re-election, but life went on at a leisurely pace, away from work. There were weekly meetings of the American Men's Association in a small hotel, a chance to touch base and eat hamburgers together, and the bowling club at Awali always had its share of American families, wearing brightly coloured shirts and clutching beers as the balls rumbled down the lanes and the skittles crashed.

The United States Navy was represented by Vice-Admiral Duke Bayne, a Commander of the Middle East Force, based on his flag-ship, the USS *La Salle*, a large, ungainly and unarmed support ship permanently moored at Mina Sulman deep water jetty and which had certainly never seen or heard a shot fired in anger. And never would. Bayne was of a different hue to Jo. Quiet, softly spoken and courteous, he was an old-style gentleman, a navy man through and through, and widely respected.

There was Louie Giacona, the gravel-voiced head of Taylor Diving from Texas, whose chequered career had included a spell as a Las Vegas pit boss. The chain-smoking Giacona was to become a particular friend and we would sit in his office, sipping beer from his little fridge as he described the merits of his latest girlfriend.

Gay Welsh and Harry Jarnagan had come to the Gulf with the oil business and stayed on to set up their own company with a local merchant, providing support services to the world of petroleum. Awalco became a success story that made them millions. 'When we started,' Welsh drawled, 'one of the top local merchant traders told me, "You won't survive, we'll drive you out of business". I told him, "We'll get up earlier than you and we'll finish later".' It was a hard-working formula that paid off; by the time I met Welsh, his partner Jarnagan was in more or less permanent retirement on a Greek island, and I never saw him. The business was run by Milby Pickell, a Texan seemingly seven feet tall and with enormous feet. Milby was a gallant southern gentleman; I helped him and his lovely brunette wife Martha celebrate when their long-awaited first child arrived.

Then there were the whistle-stoppers. The American humorist S. J. Perelman spent a fleeting visit in Bahrain, re-enacting his own version of *Around The World in Eighty Days*. Perelman, writing a flying column of his adventures for the *New Yorker*, met me in the gardens of the British Residency; he did not say anything funny. But he did agree to pose with a pith sun helmet that our enterprising occasional photographer Bob Paterson had brought along. He wouldn't wear it, but the picture made our front page.

Chester Partridge stayed briefly, to open an office for Superior Oil, his stateside overlords convinced that the sea around the island still had something to yield. 'They won't find anything,' said Jo. And they didn't. Chester – 'Roly' as he was known – passed his busy days swimming with his secretary and otherwise doing nothing, but with humour and gusto and I was sad to see him go.

Permanently in Bahrain was Frank Jerall, who handled relations with ministers, merchants and the ruling family for Brown and Root, the offshore construction group based in Houston. Poor Frank could have his patience sorely tried. A PR fireman blew in from head office on a familiarisation visit. Coarse and foul-mouthed, he embarrassed the gentle Frank greatly with his constant quest for 'poontang', when he was not managing to offend just about every merchant he came into contact with. Frank's normal composure had dropped when I met him again. 'What an asshole,' he complained. 'I have had to apologise to just about everyone he met.' Fortunately, such patently square pegs were rare.

And then there were the trouble-shooters. Lloyd Amos, a vice-president of Kaiser, a partner in the Aluminium Bahrain smelter, dropped in, bringing his own brand of bluff, no-nonsense business-speak probably better summed up as bull. But behind the face, 'Two Gun' Amos was really a giant pussycat and when he got his talk of big Kaiser expansion plans off his broad chest, was the nicest of men. What did impress me, as he spoke at a press conference, were the unopened boxes of Havana Upmann cigars piled in front of him – Castro's cigars were on the blacklist in the United States. Clearly a man who does not do things by halves, I decided. Amos in due course retired to California, to run a walnut farm. I pitied the walnut trees that failed to deliver their full production quota.

CHAPTER TWELVE

Bahrain's soaring temperatures seemed to have a similar effect on the libido, with some western expatriates exhibiting an un-inhibited promiscuity which manifested itself in short-lived affairs and – for cuckolded husbands – long-lived enmities. The Arabs looked on uncomprehending at this lack of morality among couples. Not that some were beyond a certain dalliance themselves.

One lesser Bahraini merchant complained bitterly to me about his English girlfriend. The circumstances were slightly bizarre; he had met the girl, a strikingly beautiful brunette, in London. She readily jumped at the chance of an air ticket for a holiday in 'beautiful Bahrain'. Everything was laid on, but it was not quite what she had been expecting: she was driven to one of his flats, shabby and dusty, in a back area of Manama; there, she was kept under lock and key until the evenings when he would come round in his smart air-conditioned Mercedes and they would hit the town. Beyond midnight, like Cinderella, she would be returned to her secure accommodation – so he thought – and he would dutifully go home to his unsuspecting wife and family.

But the young lady, stunning in a small brown bikini when I later met her on a local beach, was not without resource. She discovered she had a neighbour in the flat above, a good-looking and muscular Briton working on the rigs. Her door lock proved no problem for this particular Romeo and daytimes of unbridled passion followed as he spent his week off-duty in a manner probably beyond his wildest dreams. Alas for my friend the merchant, his own trysts were short-lived. He arrived one evening to find the bird had flown.

For the Bahrainis, sex and love were a private matter, conducted behind closed doors; titillation was not part of life, unless one included the traditional dancing boys who would sometimes appear after a large banquet – men only, of course – to writhe and sway to the rhythmic music from traditional players who would spend an hour tuning their instruments, warming the drum skins before a charcoal fire to ensure tautness. I saw one elderly musician so overcome by a particular performance that he seized the dancer, hair slicked back and face made-up, clasping his arms round him and planting a kiss full on the lips. The boy's face was expressionless.

Desire in this hot house for the sexes flourished. There was the brittle Home Counties wife, very upper middle class, and her husband, a considerable number of years older, a bristly, very correct ex-military man. I would see them at cocktail parties, the perfect couple, or so it seemed. But who knows what goes on behind closed doors? Living above the couple was a single man, his wife and family safely back in England. Temptation proved too much. In the early afternoons, with the husband fast sleep after the ritual gin and tonics, she would slip out and mount the stairs for an hour of wild, abandoned sex. This pattern continued for several years until it became more or less open knowledge, except to the husband of course, for in Bahrain there were few secrets.

But for the lady, it was difficult to remain dispassionate about what, for her neighbour, was a convenient arrangement with no strings attached. She fell in love. She confided in my wife, complaining sadly that her own deep feelings were not reciprocated. For the man upstairs was never likely to break with his real partner. But this spirited lady was not to be corralled; years later she ran off with the head of one of Britain's blue-chip companies, Bahrain branch.

For European marriages, Bahrain could prove a graveyard. Countless couples would tell me: 'Our marriage had been going through a bad patch; we decided to give it one last chance by coming to Bahrain.' With that sort of background, such marriages rarely survived. In truth, for many Britons, fresh from modest jobs and a dreary lifestyle, the temptations could prove too much. The island offered almost everything that money could buy, and most expatriates had that money. As Christine famously remarked: 'In the Gulf, everybody is somebody.' Sooner or later, these contract workers would return home, back to reality and obscurity.

Then there were the sad cases of European girls who had met and married Bahrainis. Many of these marriages proved wretchedly unhappy; the sophisticated handsome Arab they had met changed, back in his own country, to a very different person, traditional, naturally, and the veneer of westernisation proved to be just that. The only such marriages that seemed to thrive were those where the wife had a dominant, strong-willed personality more than capable of dealing with a husband's foibles. Staff at the British Agency, forerunner to the embassy, grew used to fielding complaints from bitterly disillusioned English girls. 'We can't help,' one attaché said to me. 'In many cases they are no longer British citizens. All we can do is offer tea and sympathy.'

The Bahrainis themselves were not above a leg pull when it came to sex, sometimes cruelly so. A lesser merchant, long married but childless, was the butt of many jokes from friends. One day a member of his regular Thursday night group, recently returned from England, rang to say that he had sent him a present from London. 'What is it?' he asked. 'It's a surprise. I've posted it to you,' he was told. The man waited in expectation. Then, one morning, he received a call from the customs department. 'Are you expecting something?' he was asked. 'Yes, I am.' 'We don't normally allow imports like this into the country, unless you can assure me you have a need for it.' The wretched man, beside himself with excitement, protested that he did indeed have a very dire need for it. The voice at the other end of the phone was sympathetic. 'In that case, I'm prepared to make an exception. You can come along and pick it up.'

Minutes later, the merchant was at the vast customs shed and ringing the bell of the duty officer. The package was handed to him in silence. He turned away, tearing at the wrapping paper. A box appeared, containing a very large vibrator. They were still laughing about it years later.

Even Ralph Izzard was not immune from embarrassment. I met him one morning looking considerably shaken. 'My dear chap, I've just had a dreadful experience, but I'm afraid I can't possibly talk about it.' As a practised newspaperman, I soon wheedled it out of him. Ralph, ever the perfect if very heterosexual gentleman – indeed, one of his early conquests had been Marianne Hoppe, the celebrated German lieder singer, in pre-war Germany – had been to a cocktail party the previous evening where he had fallen into conversation with a junior diplomat from, shall we say, the Horn of Africa.

The diplomat gave Ralph a lift home and was inevitably invited in for a nightcap before going on his way. The whisky and water duly consumed, he left. It was late, but as Ralph got ready for bed his door bell rang. Grumbling, he went to the door and looked out. There stood the diplomat, slightly apologetic, and asked if he might have just one more drink, supplies being slightly short at his home. 'Well, all right,' said Ralph ungraciously, 'but only one. I've just taken a sleeping pill and I want to go to bed.' He led the returned visitor back into his majlis area, seating him at his work table, and disappeared into the kitchen to get two more whiskies.

'I had noticed that his flies were open,' he told me. 'I thought it slightly strange. Then, as I put down the drinks and took a seat, I suddenly saw this enormous python rear up on the opposite side of the table.' Izzard was aghast. 'What did you say?' I asked. 'What could I say? I looked at him and said, "My dear chap, I'm afraid you're making a dreadful mistake".'

The same Bahraini merchant whose imported girlfriend had

absconded also complained to me about the offshore tenant of one of his crumbling flats. Waterbeds, a growing trend in the United States, had begun to make an appearance in Bahrain. 'We landlords had been concerned about the weight on the floors,' he said. 'But we never thought about leaks.' It seems that the Californian occupant, with his busty nurse girlfriend, had been romping vigorously on the mattress, creating the domestic equivalent of a choppy sea; as their passion grew, so the waves began to intensify until – Bang! – the bed exploded, subsided with the rush of a mini tsunami and the contents gushed onto the floor, along the corridor and roared down the stairwell with the force of, well, a tidal wave. The landlord was left with the bill.

In the same block of flats there lived another lusty young Briton, away for much of the time working on drilling rigs. His time spent ashore brought moments of unbridled passion. The preferred place for him and his large Scottish girlfriend was the kitchen. On the table, to be exact. As they coupled frequently during the day, his neighbours in the block opposite were taken aback to see his white naked bottom, standing out above a pair of deeply suntanned muscular legs and back, going hammer and tongs while all that could be seen of the lady were her podgy legs waving in the air. This happened with such great frequency that a secretary who lived across the courtyard and had literally a window seat, began fending off requests for seats for the daily matinee performance.

I recounted this with some hilarity to a young Bahraini friend who was an officer in the police force. 'I can beat that,' he said. 'We were called out one morning to a flat rented by an American and his lady. They had been occupying a double bed which during the day was folded back into the wall.' Their bouncing on the bedsprings somehow triggered the folding mechanism and the bed, plus easy riders, slowly upended and folded itself into the wall. There it stuck. Their muffled cries were eventually heard, the police were called, and after much wrenching and crunching with a crowbar and pickaxe, they were pulled free unhurt, but with their dignity severely compromised.

For some living alone, the imagination – and the libido – could combine in a sexual fantasyland under the relentless heat and work pressures. I used to see two grizzled Texans, both in their early sixties and wearing stetsons, as they stumped bow-legged along the streets, window-shopping. One night, when I was at a hotel nightclub with my wife for the unmissable performance by the resident singer, a large Spanish lady with an enormous décolletage, scarcely contained, the two lovelorn Lone Rangers off a drill platform were sitting at the next table, spellbound. *Maggie May* by Rod Stewart and *Chirpy Chirpy Cheep Cheep* by Middle of the Road were hot favourites then in Britain's Top of the Pops but the chanteuse's repertoire was not so ambitious and she stuck to safer numbers like her party piece, *I Never Promised You a Rose Garden*, which topped the US country charts in 1970. After watching her in silence for ten minutes, one turned to the other and confided – it must be said – in a loud voice: 'I'd suck those tits for an hour before screwing her.' Whatever gets you through the night, or, in their case, their bored time ashore as enforced bachelors.

When it came to sex, variety could be the spice of life. A coterie of lesbians made their appearance, a posse of girls working as secretaries and mostly provided by a British recruitment agency. They took jobs with companies throughout the island, local as well as foreign. They were mostly British, but there were also Dutch and German girls, some of them bisexual with occasional boyfriends. They were for the most part lipstick lesbians, with the more hardcore close-cropped hair and severe clothes limited to just one or two. One, a dark-haired petite girl who was personal secretary to a prominent Bahraini merchant, was always sweetness and light when I would see her on my way in to chat with her boss. But she had a dark side. A young British technician, quite a lothario in his way despite being very publicly married, managed to secure a date with her when the coast was clear and his wife was back in England. 'I thought I had it cracked,' he told me. 'She invited me back to her apartment and we started getting down to business. Then she opened the door of her closet. Inside was an array of whips, canes, rubber headmasks and bondage gear. She thrashed me black and blue. I left with a mass of welts and bruises – she even drew blood.' A sadder and wiser man, perhaps, but I did not notice that this particular philanderer mended his ways. As an electrician, he should have learned not to confuse his A/C with D/C.

These birds of passage, so they proved, who had alighted on Bahrain during a prolonged migration from their homes, eventually took flight again. This time their destination was Brussels, to secretarial jobs with the European Commission, and the clouds of ennui which they had helped to clear during their sojourn again closed in behind them.

Newcomers to Bahrain ranged from the ordinary to the exotic, and in this latter category surely must fit the talented Sara Leighton, a highly-respected society portrait painter from London. Titian-haired, vivacious and flirtatious, she took the island by storm, meeting in a short space of time all the movers and shakers, many of whom provided her with commissions. Through her young sister, married to a thrusting young businessman, Bob Storey, she had an entrée to all the top parties, and many Bahrainis who should have known better fell under her powerful allure. It was never clear why the gifted Sara came to spent some months in Bahrain – there were stories of a little local difficulty back in Britain, when she deemed it wise to make herself scarce – but she brightened up many a dull evening at those interminable cocktail parties, drawing men to her like a magnet, while wives seethed in the background.

Such was her personality that she even persuaded one young Briton, David Goode, a chartered accountant with the Indian-owned department store of Jashanmal's, to change his smart and immaculately-parted hairstyle. The next time I saw David, normally a conservative pinstriped figure, his dark wavy hair was transformed into an incongruous busby, bursting out of his skull on both sides and resembling more a New Guinea head-hunter than the sober businessman he really was.

In reality, Sara promised more than she gave, and despite her assiduous working of the decision-makers, she made sure there was never any scandal attached to her. She really was in a class of her own. Even Louie Giacona, boss of the local branch of the Houston company Taylor Diving, and no mean judge of horse flesh, had to concede: 'That is one helluva dame.' Her exile from Britain proved short-lived, and she vanished from Bahrain as suddenly as she had appeared, leaving behind tantalising memories and a clutch of portraits that, for all I know, hang on the walls of homes in Bahrain to this day.

Girls came, and girls went. One, straight from the Home Counties in England, all cut-glass accent and exclusive school, arrived to spend a few days and thought she had snared a prestige prize in the form of a member of the ruling family. Within weeks she was seen very publicly at the wheel of a Mercedes-Benz sports car, and on his arm at local hotels. But if she thought she was smart, her beau, married with children and the head of a government department, was smarter. The car was only ever on loan and when he wearied of her, back it went and off she went.

There could be exceptions. One, a blonde Scandinavian, met her Bahraini 'husband' in Europe. 'I thought he was a handsome Italian,' she told me. They became an item and eventually moved to Saudi Arabia where her partner, reluctant to move back home, took a nondescript job. He began to spend more and more time across the water in Bahrain on his weekends; he returned one day to announced that he had become married. The dismayed lady nevertheless moved to Bahrain too, where for the next few years she had the unofficial position of Wife No 2. A bitter-sweet lady, and a cautionary tale to others tempted to follow in her footsteps.

The small contingent of air stewardesses on the twin-turbo-prop Fokker Friendships with which Gulf Air plied its local routes also had to be diplomats in those early days. Sometimes the aisle would be jammed with hunting parties, hooded falcons held on their handlers' gloved mits, after an aircraft had to be summarily taken from service on the demand of a ruler who had suddenly decided on a whim on a hunting trip in pursuit of the giant bustard in Pakistan. From the surreal to the down to earth. It was not unknown for Bedu women, unused to twentieth-century travel and baffled by sanitary arrangements, to attempt to squat in the hand basins in the toilets.

Before the home-grown airline had mushroomed into wide-body jet expansion, these imported stewardesses provided a certain amount of diversion for those on the ground. While the phrase 'a man in every port' would be too sweeping, certainly there were those who did bestow their favours with generosity, with admirers in a host of destinations. But unlike many cabin staff who were later recruited literally in scores, they were troupers, and the many affaires were matched with a large degree of discretion. What happened outside Bahrain stayed outside Bahrain, for the most part.

What was it about Bahrain? Was it the climate, or something in the air? What made people behave in ways they would never have contemplated back at home? Perhaps it was the excitement of living in foreign parts; perhaps it was the money; perhaps, with so much attention, they believed themselves possessed of an allure they had never before dreamt of. Perhaps it really was a case of, 'in the Gulf, everybody is somebody'.

CHAPTER THIRTEEN

In the non-stop toil of producing this fledgling newspaper, one of the key props was the veteran Ralph Izzard, with a lifetime's experience of the world's hot spots. He belonged to that rare breed, the truly professional reporter whose dedication above all else was to the story, to that buzz of snatching an exclusive under the eyes of the rival press pack and then beating them to the wire office.

As a rolling stone, he somehow came to rest in Bahrain after some years running his own cine company, a time of much hard work for very little reward, he told me. The birth of the *Gulf Mirror* was a heaven-sent opportunity to supplement his monthly pay cheques from the *Financial Times* and the news agency Agence France Presse.

During long, languid evenings in his courtyard, under the stars, Ralph would yarn and I would listen, while in the background his record player would work its way through a selection from the stash of old 78 discs he had discovered in the suq, unused and in their original brown paper sleeves: classics, jazz, and memorably, the incomparable Australian baritone Peter Dawson. A particular favourite with Ralph was *The Road to Mandalay*, with the words by Kipling and sung to a tinny piano accompaniment. Dawson's rich voice would boom out, often competing with the call to prayer, no doubt to the irritation of his Arab neighbours over the wall.

His own life story was like something out of a *Boy's Own* adventure. You couldn't have made it up. Ralph really was a living legend. He got into journalism by the back door, literally. After coming down from Cambridge with a degree in estate management – 'never the slightest use to me' – his father Percy, for years the gardening correspondent of the *Daily Mail*, managed to secure him a job as a cleaner in the Berlin office; this was the Depression and jobs were like hens' teeth.

He graduated to reporting and soon became the office's number two. For a young man, Berlin was a vibrant, decadent city in the early days of Nazi Germany. The social whirl of masked balls and parties was non-stop if you had the stamina. Ralph, slim and good-looking, proved to be a Lothario. An early conquest was Marianne Hoppe, the actress and classical lieder singer, later to become a household name in Europe, whose admirers included Adolf Hitler – he even invited her to dinner.

The young British journalist, now fluent in German, moved on and became engaged to the daughter of a Prussian general. The regular Sunday lunches were an ordeal for Izzard. He was obliged to play war games with his future father-in-law, using models. 'It was something I never got the hang of,' he confessed to me. 'I will never forget the old gentleman staring at me, aghast. "Vot, Herr Izzard, you are bringing up howitzers to destroy a bicycle platoon?" '

At Cambridge Ralph had become a keen amateur boxer. Indeed, he narrowly missed going into the ring with Oxford's champion, Wilfred Thesiger, later a celebrated explorer famous for crossing the Empty Quarter of Saudi Arabia by camel with Bedu companions. Ralph just escaped being drawn against Thesiger, tall, gangling and decidedly weedy-looking. But he packed a terrific punch. His opponent, Cambridge's best, barely lasted one round. 'When I finally woke up, I was walking down the street to the pub with fellow team-members,' he told Ralph.

In his spare time Ralph would train in a local Berlin gym and was sometimes picked to spar with Max Schmeling, who achieved rock-star status in Germany after beating Joe Louis to win the world heavyweight title in 1930. 'All the pros knew that when you sparred with amateurs you didn't rough them up,' he recalled to me. 'But Max must have got out of bed on the wrong side one day.

He started to knock me about quite considerably. As I went to my corner I thought, I'm not putting up with this. When we came out again, I met him with a whirling bolo punch which I deliberately threw low, right into his crutch.' The world champion sank to the canvas, his face contorted with pain. Ralph fussed over him. 'My dear Max, I am so sorry, I do apologise.'

His ability to defend himself did land him in some scrapes, all accepted as a matter of course by the capital's international press corps. But the serious business of work did occasionally intervene, and he got to know well many of the Nazi leaders. 'Goering (chief of the Luftwaffe) quite liked me.' But Goebbels, the poisonous head of Hitler's propaganda machine, took a dislike to him. He never met the Fuhrer.

Ralph was off-duty and at a masked ball when one of the biggest stories broke. The head of his office, 'an effete little gay', lived in some splendour in a baroque apartment opposite the Reichstag. He was hosting a twee little dinner party when the phone rang. It was the London news desk wanting details of a reported fire at . . . the Reichstag. The desk was reassured that a fire simply wasn't possible. But throughout the evening, from the soup course through to liqueurs, the calls from a frantic London news editor kept on coming, their man on the spot becoming increasingly irate. With the last conversation, with news that fire engines from miles away were being called to Berlin, what was left of his composure deserted him. 'You've ruined my evening,' he stormed down the phone. 'I shall now prove to you that this story is a complete fabrication.' Theatrically, he strode to the heavy velvet curtains and wrenched them aside. He let out a shriek. Opposite him, the Reichstag blazed like a devil's inferno, torched by the Nazis in an act of provocation blamed on the communists.

In those far-off days scrapes and worse were never far away. One evening Ralph and his new German fiancee planed to visit a weight-lifting competition in a Berlin stadium. This was a prestigious event; Ralph was in black tie and his fraulein in a little black dress. 'There was a tradition that whenever a competitor advanced to the podium, a brass band would strike up his favourite tune,' Ralph explained. As the leotard-clad contenders grunted and groaned, muscles bulging as they wrenched at the giant barbell, sweat pouring off them, the band would strike up with the audience in evening dress roaring them on. Slightly surreal. But on this occasion what should have been a dignified and formal occasion descended into something worthy of the Keystone Cops.

Ralph and fraulein never made it to their seats. They arrived late, the brass band was in full blast and the little job's-worth clerk in the ticket box refused them entry, explaining that to admit them now would cause a distraction and some regional champion could be put off his performance. The discussion grew heated and ended in a tussle at the flight of stairs leading down into the bowels of the stadium. Blows were struck but the official was no match for a trained boxer and away he went, bowling down the stairs and crashing through the swing doors at the bottom.

'There was a slight pause,' Ralph recollected, 'then the doors burst open again and a squad of security men poured out, rushing upwards to deal with me.' Ralph took up a fighting stance and as the leading figure of the phalanx reached him, delivered a smashing uppercut. His target rocketed backwards, rolling down head over heels and scattering the rest of the posse like ninepins. At the bottom of the stairs they regrouped and charged back up. Force prevailed and Ralph was unceremoniously ejected. In the meantime, the bird had flown; his lady, wearying of this uncouth display, had made her departure.

The night was still young and Ralph, dishevelled and with a black eye, decided to salvage what he could of the evening and hailed a cab to take him to the press club to lick his wounds. As he entered the bar, bow-tie up around his neck and covered in dust, the staffer from the London *Daily Express* looked up. 'What on earth has happened, Izzard?' Ralph explained. 'My dear fellow, this is utterly outrageous. You represent one of the world's leading newspapers and you have been treated disgracefully. I insist you make an official complaint.'

Not without some misgivings, Ralph accompanied his helpful colleague to the local police station. The shaven-headed desk sergeant listened impassively. He painstakingly took down the details, pen scratching. Further investigation was promised. The next day, in the sober light of morning, Ralph reviewed the events. He went down to the police station. The same sergeant was still on duty. He looked up. 'Yes, Herr Izzard, what is it this time?' he asked wearily. Ralph told him that, on reflection, he had decided to withdraw his complaint. 'Very wise, Herr Izzard.'

As war loomed, Ralph was despatched by Lord Rothermere, the *Mail*'s proprietor, to Czechoslovakia where the press baron was convinced the next world conflict would begin. 'He wasn't far wrong.' And for a year he cooled his heels there, covering just two stories: the invention of a glass razor blade, and the tracking down of a serial killer.

He eventually returned to England just before war broke out, where he tried in vain to enlist. But his marriage to the Prussian general's daughter had made him suspect. He finally succeeded in joining the Royal Navy, signing on at a tiny recruiting office far from the capital. He was made a torpedo gunner's mate and posted as number two on a small gun added to the rear deck of a tanker. Back and forth they went, criss-crossing the Atlantic on the vital milk run of bringing in essential aviation fuel. 'Ships were being torpedoed by U-boats in front of us, astern and abeam, but we never got hit,' he told me during one of the many evenings spent at his house, as he reminisced over his usual whisky and water.

'I was reading the Hemingway best-seller *For Whom The Bell Tolls* in our cabin each night. My chief, the Torpedo Gunner, was a much tattooed man of advanced years who had never read a book in his life. He asked to borrow it and each night he would climb into his bunk, carefully pull on a pair of wire-rimmed glasses, and slowly turn the pages. It took him weeks. When he finally closed the book, I asked what he thought.' There was a long pause. Finally he delivered his critical view. 'That must have been a helluvva fuck,' he said thoughtfully, 'to shift the deck.'

Ralph was finally rescued from the nerve-wracking tedium of those long slow voyages when he was abruptly summoned to Admiralty House in London, wearing his little sailor hat and best bell-bottomed trousers. 'Where on earth have you been, Izzard?' he was asked. 'We've been looking for you for months.' Fluent in German, he was transferred straight into the intelligence section – where he was to meet Ian Fleming, creator of James Bond – and given the rank of commander.

While in Normandy in the weeks following the D-Day landings, Ralph was attached for a while in his naval intelligence capacity to the commando brigade led by Lord Lovat, famous for raising the Lovat Scouts from his Highland estate, experts in stalking and sniping, who were taken over by the army. 'I was never very keen on Shimi Lovat. He always struck me as dangerously reckless.' Reckless he may have been, but he was also a first-class shot. 'I saw him snatch up a .303 service rifle to bring down a pheasant on the wing in France. It's hard enough to do that with a shotgun.' The respect was mutual – and Lovat was a hard man to impress. Not so with the novelist Evelyn Waugh, whose applications to join the commandos were repeatedly blocked by Lovat. 'He rather cruelly likened Waugh's appearance to that of a eunuch.'

With the war over, it was back to the *Daily Mail*. He was posted to India, where he witnessed the assassination of Mahatma Gandhi in New Delhi in 1948. He had arrived late to see Gandhi and found it was impossible to get across the packed square to join the rest of the press. He watched, over the heads of the crowds, and saw the lone gunman fire the fatal shots. The other journalists were unable to penetrate the throng in their way on that hot, dusty day, while Ralph hastened to the nearest cable office with his world exclusive.

He later covered the war in Korea but it was the Himalayas that led to him achieving international fame. He was despatched to follow the official expedition to Everest and doggedly toiled away up the foothills and lower slopes with just three sherpas, literally in the footsteps of the official expedition which numbered more than 300. *The Times* of London had bought up the rights to Colonel John Hunt's attempt on the highest mountain in the world. His climbers, who included the New Zealander Edmund Hillary – who conquered the peak with Sherpa Tenzing – had been forbidden to speak to any other journalists.

But Ralph, now famous as the mountaineer in gym shoes, sent back scoop after scoop to London of the expedition's progress, including an early snatched photograph of Hillary 'taking a breather', according to the caption. 'He was actually having a pee in the snow,' Ralph admitted. And when success was announced, in time for the 1953 coronation of Queen Elizabeth II, Hillary's determined face, all teeth, was carried in the *Mail*, again, a picture snatch. 'It was displayed throughout the country,' Ralph confessed, 'but in fact he was telling the entire nation to fuck off – that's what he said when he looked up and saw me with my camera.'

The Everest unofficial expedition led to him being sent by the *Daily Mail* to track down the fabled Yeti, the so-called Abominable Snowman, that the sherpas claimed to exist. Apart from footprints in the snow, no hard proof was ever found. When the Chinese invaded Tibet, the *Mail* sent a favoured staffer to do a first-hand piece. To help him along the mountainous route to the rooftop of the world, they brought in Ralph, with his Himalayan experience. 'We were 40 miles from the Tibetan city, Lhasa, and not even across the border, when my colleague sat in the snow and refused to go another step. "They can fire me," he said. "I can't go on." We were sitting there, wondering what to do, when a group of Tibetan refugees came stumbling along the track, fleeing their homeland. I grabbed them and we interviewed them through an interpreter.'

Thus it was that the reluctant journalist made his name with a world scoop headlined 'First Man Into Tibet', with stories of burning buildings, bullets and bloodshed. 'In fact, he never even crossed the border.'

When he finally left the *Mail*, with an enhanced severance pay negotiated directly with Lord Rothermere himself, Ralph arrived in Bahrain after his brief flirtation with the film-making business. He moved into his delightful Persian house with Charlie, his African grey parrot purchased from a crew member on the dhow quay. Charlie was the inspiration for one of his more whimsical *Gulf Mirror* columns – and for my most risqué headline, Confessions of a Feather-Plucker. Its powers of mimicry were legendary, from the pop of a beer can opening to the clack-clack-clack of Ralph's typewriter, and a dry smoker's cough as he emerged from his bedroom in the morning. And deep in Charlie's memory bank were other voices. When local painters descended on the house to whitewash the walls, their voices sparked a chord with Charlie, who had them convulsed with Arabic nautical slang, including references to the wind and the chance of finding a willing lady in port.

One of Ralph's highlights of the year was the visit of his lifelong friend Gerald Morgan Russell, scion of an American banking family, who had become almost by adoption part-English and part-French. When Gerald wasn't in New York, he lived in his French chateau, and when he wasn't there, he would winter at the palace in India of his friend the Maharajah of Jodhpur. For the unmarried Gerald, who always had a twinkle in his eye for the ladies, a diversion to Bahrain had become a habit. Gerald, courtly, urbane and somewhat irascible, as befitted a trust fund boy who had probably never done a day's work in his life, had had a distinguished war record, spending time undercover in France – he spoke French fluently. Now, as an ageing bachelor, he had become a little set in his ways, though only too willing to be led astray by Ralph. He always travelled with a balalaika on which, with bad grace, he would allow himself to be persuaded to play . . . a strumming of chords lasting perhaps 15 seconds before putting it back in its box, closing it with a snap of the fasteners and declaring: 'That's all you're hearing.'

Ralph had a relative who occupied a senior position with Bapco, and in anticipation of Gerald's arrival, they had arranged a formal dinner party with colleagues, some of them very senior. Shay Sawyer, our women's page writer, was there with her husband Tony. She described the scene. 'The dinner was for eight o'clock. But at eight there was no sign of the guest of honour. Thirty minutes later, still no sign. It got to nine o'clock and the host was visibly twitching.' Finally, at 9.30, a full hour and a half late, they heard the sound of a car as Ralph drove up to the side of the house in Awali in his decrepit American gas-guzzler.

First Ralph lurched out, then Gerald, both clearly the worse for wear. One of them walked straight through the hedge, missing the door completely. The dinner that followed was strained, and conversation spasmodic. I spoke to Gerald the next day. 'Oh, it was so boring,' he sighed. 'The only way I could deal with it was to get through a load of drink beforehand.' The dinner party host and hostess blamed Ralph, of course.

Boredom, and the avoidance of it, played a big part in Gerald's life. 'He's absolutely impossible to take shopping,' an exasperated Ralph would complain. 'We would be standing outside the super-market in town and I would say, "Now, Gerald, I just have to nip into this shop. Would you stand here holding this pound of sausages, and wait for me?" But Gerald would say, "I just can't, Izzard". Why not, I would ask. "It would be just too boring".'

Gerald was also a man of highly eccentric personal habits. Particularly concerning his daily ablutions. This used to enrage Ralph. Every morning, it seemed, Gerald would carry out a definite ritual. 'He stands on the toilet bowl, feet astride the rim, then rocks back and forth while spooning peanut butter from a jar,' said an appalled Ralph. 'Then he had the audacity to complain that my toilet was broken – his rocking had put a bloody great crack in it and I had to buy a new one.'

One of Gerald's visits coincided with the prolonged stay in Bahrain of bankers, as the island's reputation as a financial centre began to take off. Hotel space was limited and many were billeted with Ralph. The air was loud with upper-class English accents, public school guffaws and whinnying laughs. 'I'm never quite sure whether I'm playing host to the officers' mess or a junior board of spivs,' Ralph would complain.

But Gerald, as always, had the last laugh. 'The bankers were discussing personal ablutions,' Ralph explained, 'and Gerald spoke out forthrightly about standing on the toilet bowl, rocking, and of course eating the peanut butter.' 'How did they react?' I asked. 'Of course, they all agreed with him. After all, he's a multi-millionaire.'

Ralph was very much a product of the public school system in England. After his childhood prep days at the Dragon School in Oxford, he moved as a teenager to The Leys in Cambridge where one of his fellow pupils was Malcolm Lowry, later to achieve fame for his classic book *Under The Volcano*. 'Lowry (who died in 1957) has been discovered posthumously,' Ralph would muse, 'and there's a tremendous fascination about his life, particularly his early days, which no one seems to know anything about. But I do – perhaps there's a book in it and a chance to make some money.' If there was, he never pursued it further, but he did give me a little snippet about life at The Leys. 'The head was a large man much given to thrashing small boys in his study with a cane. When these punishments were meted out, his wife would suddenly appear, and watch silently.'

The head, it seemed, fancied himself as a batsman and would sometimes take over at the crease where he would strike a W. G. Grace-style pose, bat raised, instead of the usual stance of hunching over in front of the wicket. On one occasion he did just that and then called for play to resume. But the bowler in his nervousness miscalculated and delivered a yorker, the heavy leather ball bouncing high and early and cannoning under the head's guard to catch him right in his crutch. He collapsed in agony. 'As he lay groaning, all I could hear him say was "It's all over boys, it's all over," ' Ralph recalled. Lowry had a facial expression which gave the appearance of him smirking. As the stricken head lay on the grass, he caught sight of Lowry in the ring of alarmed faces looking down at him. He saw the smirk, mistakenly thought Lowry was enjoying the moment and howled 'Boy, in my study. Immediately!' Lowry was led off and no doubt chastised severely, under the gloating eye of the head's wife.

Ralph's annual leave during the first year of production of the *Gulf Mirror* came at a time when I had managed to change the office's postal box; the tiny steel cube among scores of similar ones set in the post office wall in the centre of town was simply not big enough to take our growing weekly mail. Ricky Thorpe, the Post Master, allocated me a much larger one, and with a different number. But I forgot to tell Ralph, who had promised to mail his usual column from England. As each week passed with no sign of his copy, I grew increasingly concerned and the newspaper had to publish a note: 'Ralph Izzard is away on leave. His column will resume on his return.'

I then had to make a quick trip to Kuwait as the guest of Rothman's, the cigarette people who were taking part in a large exhibition. Basil Everett, British representative of their Gulf office, knew how to entertain and that first night we all sat down to a sumptuous banquet at a leading hotel, where drink – whisky, I recall – was served discreetly at the side of the table from a teapot, Kuwait being officially 'dry'. I awoke next morning with a splitting headache. As I tried to gather my thoughts, the phone on the bedside table rang. It was Ralph.

'I've been in touch with the office and I gather you're anxious to make contact,' he began. As we spoke, two things were uppermost in my mind: the line was bad, his voice faint and this was a connection that easily be cut off; the other was a very urgent desire to urinate, after a night of over-indulgence. What to do. I knew that if I asked him to hang on while I dodged into the bathroom, he might think I had gone and hang up. My eyes glanced on the tray of morning coffee that had just been delivered. Deliverance. As we spoke, I seized the small coffee pot and filled it, then the milk jug, then the sugar bowl and, finally, the coffee cup itself. With no sign of the torrent being staunched, I finally had to take the risk and left Ralph hanging on while I concluded the operation in the bathroom. Mercifully, he was still there when I emerged, and we were able to solve the riddle of the missing columns. Back in Bahrain, our old postal box was crammed with them.

Ralph's journey back to Bahrain some weeks later included a moment of high drama. With the aircraft only thirty minutes out of Beirut, a fault was detected. The crew went into full emergency mode as the 707 circled, using up the last of its fuel before the final approach over the sea to the runway. Passengers were instructed to remove shoes and spectacles and lean forward in their seats, arms over the heads, as the emergency landing went ahead. 'I checked my pulse,' Ralph said later. 'To my surprise, it was perfectly normal. There was an overlarge Lebanese lady in the seat directly in front me. As we made our final approach, all I could think of was the prospect of being thrust into eternity via her enormous backside.' In the event, the aircraft touched down without incident. Even for Ralph, it had been an anxious moment.

CHAPTER FOURTEEN

A peaceful place though Bahrain was, there could be stormy weather, and demonstrations could break out, quickly becoming menacing. These would usually be short-lived but not always so. We had been on the island only a few weeks when unrest flared. There had been growing complaints about, of all things, the price of bread: the cost of the flat, unleavened loaves produced at small street-corner beehive ovens fired by gas, which are to be seen all over the island.

The circular dough is slapped on the smooth walls inside the ovens using a cloth-covered mushroom-shaped piece of wood and then picked off with a metal spike when ready. Such bread is a staple in the diet of just about all Bahraini families. And so the protests grew. Other grievances then surfaced and nightly from our house we could hear villagers being hectored by local leaders, their comments amplified through ramshackle loudspeaker systems.

The trouble was like a volcano about to erupt. Suddenly, one day, work stopped and demonstrators took to the streets. A mob formed in Manama, swelled by more and more recruits as it passed through the city centre. The faint muttering heard in the distance grew to a growl, and then a full-throated roar as the crowd surged nearer. As worried shopkeepers peered from their doors, an advance guard of marchers ran ahead, calling into each shop, warning them to close or risk breakages. And so another noise was added to the growing hubbub, the rattle of steel blinds being hurriedly slammed down over shop windows.

The police were not slow to react. They had had plenty of experience, and expatriates in their cars were pulled over and told to avoid trouble spots. As one spearhead of the crowd broke away to advance on Government House, the heavy gates were swung shut and then came the pop-pop-pop of tear-gas shells being fired. Solicitous police officers stationed further along the seafront dual-carriageway handed out tissues to Christine as, eyes streaming, she beat a hasty retreat at the wheel of her car.

Such outbreaks were very much a part of the Bahraini character, a slow-burning grievance that suddenly boils over and then ends, seemingly as quickly as it began. But things could get nasty, there could be outbreaks of violence, and then the riot squad would be called in. These were definitely the heavies, recruited from Baluchistan, tall, strong men helmeted and in protective clothing, carrying the heavy, long cane lathis and plastic shields. From a safe distance, I watched them form up, under a barrage of missiles, stones, bricks and pieces of breeze-block.

In charge was a Welsh police officer, with the full-time job of training his men though sometimes they would not be deployed on the streets for up to two years. And this was when the full-on months of hard physical preparation paid off. His line of men stood motionless as stones and bottles bounced off the shields. Once they were rushed, but the mob was beaten back with painful thwacks from the lathis. Then the line of police began to move, corralling the mob, closing off streets and driving a wedge into the crowd. Soon it began to thin out as protestors melted away. And suddenly it was all over for the day. But this particular protest rumbled on for three more days, and detachments of the Bahrain Defence Force were brought in, with armoured cars parked on roundabouts, engines rumbling, and sentries stationed opposite all roads.

The tension felt across Bahrain collapsed like a pricked balloon. The point had been made; a government subsidy helped cushion the rise in the price of bread – caused by soaring costs of imported flour – and peace broke out, to the great relief of everyone living in Manama. The ringleaders were jailed briefly and it was back to business for the merchants. And the riot control officer, exhausted from nights without sleep and his body a mass of bruises from head to foot, from accurately aimed missiles, kicks and punches, was sent away to an exotic location for a little rest and recuperation.

But for most of the time the Bahrainis were a gentle, peace-loving people. Yet if they happened to be in the wrong place at the wrong time, they could expect to be roughly handled by police. One young merchant told me indignantly how he had become caught up in the crowd and been arrested, showing his bruises from his struggle with burly police. Angrily, he sought an audience with the prime minister, Sheikh Khalifa, and complained bitterly. The quietly spoken Sheikh Khalifa, ever a model of courtesy and concern, was sympathetic. 'They tear and we must mend,' he said of the police. Mollified, the young man took his leave. But the message was clear: the Arab steel fist is concealed in a velvet glove.

I seemed to manage no more than one day off work a week, and that was Sunday; take away the usual visit to the palace at Rifa'a, and then lunch at the Rotary Club, a chore, but a very necessary one – anyone of consequence who passed through the sheikhdom was a guest – and much of the day was gone. As a family, we organised beach barbecues and then more private ones, when Anwar Abdul-Rahman, the paper's circulation magician, gave us the use of his garden along Budaiya's lush fertile strip, on the north-east coast, which came with date palms, a little house and a small swimming pool. To fill it, one had to start the Lister diesel pump at the side; as it coughed into life, nothing would happen for a few seconds. Then, wonder of wonders, a gush of ice-cold water would jet out of the pipe and into the pool, straight from the artesian supply many feet underground. We had the luxury of swimming in a bitingly cold pool before it slowly warmed in the 100 degree-plus sun. The artesian supply is now gone, lowered for ever by the demands made on it, replaced by desalinated supplies – when we arrived, our drinking water came out of a dirty, rusting delivery tanker from Manama's ice-making plant. Fortunately, it never seemed to do us any harm.

The word garden was something of a misnomer to Britons on the island, as these have little in common with the neat, manicured flower beds of the home counties. To an Arab, and especially for a Persian, the word means a walled area – ensuring privacy – with ranks of date palms, below them beds of soil with raised earth banks, in which a variety of produce is grown, from onions to melons. Nightly they are flooded from a central cistern, the chuckle of running water a low murmur beneath the creaking of the palm fronds. Such gardens evoked a strong emotional response from the Bahrainis, and indeed the word Eden, believed to derive from Persian, meaning garden, has the same meaning for Arabs and Aryans alike: paradise.

They were an idyllic setting for long lazy afternoons, with smoke drifting across from a barbecue and dips in a swimming pool to cool off. But even paradise can have its flaws. In one garden we visited there was a caged enclosure which contained two baboons. Our daughters were warned in no uncertain terms not to go near them. Towards the end of the afternoon I heard a howl, and knew immediately what had happened. Rushing round to the cage, I saw one of my girls, ashen faced, nursing a bleeding arm. She insisted she had hurt herself on a piece of wood with a nail in it. But the two puncture marks on her forearm told a different story, and matched the long incisors of a baboon. Jumping into the car, I drove her quickly to the American Mission Hospital in Manama, where she was stitched and then given all the necessary jabs and a few more besides by a very concerned doctor. There were no after-effects, mercifully. We heard later that in the minutes before she had approached the cage to feed the baboons, two little boys had been teasing them. And when she thrust a banana between the bars, they were in no mood for any generosity. She bears two tiny white scars on the inside of her left arm to this day.

There was drama of another sort one afternoon when I had been driving the family home from our weekly shopping trip to the local supermarket. As I motored down the dual carriageway, not a thought in my mind, the head of a horse, nostrils flared and ornate bridle flailing, suddenly appeared above the rosy pink flowers of the oleanders that lined the central reservation. It was surreal, high speed and yet also in slow motion. The rest of the horse, a handsome white stallion, burst through the bushes directly in front of my car. Horrified, I knew I had to take desperate, quick action. My immediate fear was that if the horse rolled onto the bonnet, a hoof was likely to come through the windscreen and strike a passenger – Christine was in the front seat, the girls in the back. Fatalities, when motorists collided with a camel elsewhere in the Gulf, were all too common.

Trying to think at the speed of light, I knew that if I stamped hard on the brakes there was no telling what the car would do, possibly swerve and flip on its back. Instinct took over. I dabbed the brakes of the Japanese saloon and estimated that, as the bolting horse crossed our path, there was room for the car to slide past. It was perfect timing; we should have been lucky. But at the last split second the frenzied horse suddenly turned its head, saw the car and reared. We struck it on the flank with a bang, half knocking it to its knees. But we were unhurt and as I pulled over, the stallion, all thoughts of flight now gone, stood bleeding at the roadside, gasping and trembling. With Christine as white as a sheet and the children shocked, I drove on the half-mile to a large police station. Jumping out, I quickly explained what had happened to the sergeant behind the desk. 'You must make a written report,' he said without looking up.

We went straight home where I immediately made a phone call to a fellow Briton, a vet, who patched up the thoroughbred, which thankfully made a full recovery. I found out later that it had been in the care of brothers in a nearby suburb, had broken free and then bolted. And there was an interesting postscript. Some time later I received a demand for damages; the stallion, it transpired, belonged to a member of the ruling family and was valuable. I ignored this vexatious threat of litigation and heard no more of it.

One weekend, there was the novelty for me of a camping trip to the desert area south of the island, as the guest of a local politician in the Ruler's home township of Rifa'a. This was no backpacking expedition. We were borne out to the dunes by chauffeur-driving limousines, the baggage being brought up by jeep. Garish ridge tents were erected, a fire built from dried bushes and a brass coffee pot placed on the embers. Then we sat back on rugs and cushions, under the stars, and waited for our dinner. And waited, and waited. Finally it arrived – on the back of a flat-bed truck from a village miles away, the rice and meat still piping hot in the huge drum-like cooking utensils. And as a meal, it was as good as any I had ever had.

To sleep on, I had brought a sun-lounger from our roof terrace which had seen better days, and I stretched out on it as the smoke from the dying fire drifted into our tent. There was a rude awakening. Around three o'clock, the fabric on my lounger suddenly gave way with a large ripping sound, depositing me on the Persian carpet that covered the sand. I lay there, my head still upright on the pillow and my feet sticking up on the bottom of the now useless frame. Awkwardly, I rolled off, aware of the possibility of scorpions, and my foot nudged a sleeping companion, snoring loudly. He did not stir. I rolled myself into my blanket and curled up in a ball on top of the rug, sleeping fitfully until morning, when the clang of a pestle on mortar announced the preparation of coffee and the start of a new day. As we waited for the clink of cups heralding the first brew, I discreetly folded up the treacherous sun-lounger and cast it quietly behind a nearby bush.

Far away, near exposed sandbanks glistening with dried salt, flamingos by the score delicately waded at the edge of the sea, their pink foliage resplendent in the early morning sun. We had been promised a hunting trip, to take advantage of the migrating winter wildfowl settling on narrow strips of sand at the water's edge. There was one shotgun, a Browning pump-action with its barrel streaked with rust. Any duck we saw was up and away, well out of range as we approached, splashing through the shallows. Finally, a lone cormorant unwisely ventured too close. The two shots were wide and it veered off. Others, disturbed, sped over our heads like low missiles, to be greeted by more shots. All missed. My host was unworried. 'They're impossible to eat any way,' he said. 'They just taste of fish.' As a wildfowling safari, it was a disaster. As an out-of-the-ordinary experience, the weekend was memorable.

Looking for some other form of diversion, I thought of a boat. I consulted Salem Al-Absy, the wise private secretary to the Prime Minister, later to be Bahrain's ambassador to Jordan. His family were from Hidd, the tiny fishing village with houses clustered on the southernmost tip of Muharraq, ringed by the semi-circular fish traps whose ownership was jealously guarded and handed down, father to son. Salem located a small huri, teak-built, about 12 feet long, sharp-ended fore and aft, with sails. It had been used by two Muharraqis who went pearl-diving in the shallows; palm-front matting lined the inside timbers and it was big enough for them to sleep in it at night. Salem's cousin Eid Abdulla Yousuf, later to become Harbourmaster, sailed it over to the Mina Sulman jetty.

I swapped the lateen sails for a two-stroke outboard and we spent many happy hours afloat. But first came the maiden voyage, which it turned out could well have been my only voyage. I was unused to boats of any description and similarly unfamiliar with the technicalities of an engine. I set off alone early one Sunday morning and rapidly was forced to confront my own utter lack of competence at that early stage. The little huri was moored at a small jetty in the port area. I manhandled the ridiculously heavy 5hp British Anzani outboard over the edge of the quay and secured it to the stern. A group of off-duty marine police officers, lounging on a patrol launch tied up at the next berth, watched me out of idleness as they smoked. I cast off, then fumbled with the engine's pull-cord and tugged it sharply several times. Nothing. I grinned at my audience, primed the engine again, and then yanked the cord vigorously, rewrapping it around the engine spool each time. The engine resolutely refused to fire.

By this time I had drifted past the launch and I could see choppy water in the large partially-enclosed lagoon, with the rough waters of the sea beyond. Feigning nonchalance, despite a mounting panic, I stepped into the middle of the boat, unshipped the large crude oars, made them fast to the makeshift rowlocks, and began attempts to row. My craft continued to drift; abandoning the attempts at the oars, I sprang back onto the tiny rear deck, seized the pull-cord again and yanked it repeatedly. Not once did the little engine emit such as a cough. My boat was now pitching alarmingly as the swell began to hit it, the audience of police was still watching disinterestedly and I was heading for the open sea, if not up shit creek without a paddle, then definitely up shit creek without an engine.

Nearly a quarter of a mile away was the line of railings marking a skeleton pier with a walkway on top. My little boat rolled and tossed as it slowly drifted toward this hope of haven. Half an hour later I was there, my huri rocking alarmingly and uncontrollably. I leapt out, tied up the boat to a metal stanchion and walked hurriedly along the walkway to where I could see the offices of the Bahrain Ship-Repair Yard. I entered, and saw one of the British managers, Andy Hunter, sitting at his desk. He looked up in surprise, produced a cup of coffee and we exchanged pleasantries as we passed the time of day. Through the window I could see the tall prow of my huri rearing up and down out of the water like a demented horse, being slammed against the railings; I even imagined that I could hear the teak splintering.

Finally Andy, dapper in shorts and long stockings, said: 'Well, what brings you here?' I hurriedly explained. 'No problem,' he said, and in less than ten minutes my unbiddable boat was under tow to the main mooring area. He readily agreed to cast a professional look at the engine, but growled dourly: 'If it takes more than half an hour, we'll charge you at the full rate.' The engine was stripped down, a fault discovered, and thereafter managed to behave itself, save for two somewhat disconcerting faults: it would never start easily, and being in fixed gear would never stop until the carburettor had exhausted itself of fuel. The British Anzani proved a robust beast, if an infuriating one, not unlike a mule. Kicks and blows never had any effect; friendly persuasion and the patience of Job were the only things that worked. My boat survived its pounding and, strangely, I did not lose my nerve. Worse things really do happen at sea.

It was a steep learning curve but the rare times at sea that I managed to have by myself I treasured. As I fished miles offshore, dolphins would pop up around the boat and play. I once heard a low groan; startled, I looked up to see an almost human face 40 yards away, staring at me. We gazed at each other, then the triangular brown form slowly slid below the surface; I had been privileged to have had a rare sighting of the famous dugong, or sea cow, known to sailors in the past as the mermaid.

Once, when I ventured several miles down the coast, near the oil wharf of Sitra, I crossed paths with a supertanker. As my little boat put-putted on its way, with me in flowing Arab gown standing on the little poop deck and steering with my bare foot on the tiller, I realised that I would be cutting things rather fine. But I also considered I had the right of way, according to the rules of the roads, a small fishing boat proceeding on its course against a behemoth pulling out from its mooring. Two huge blasts from its siren were deafening; I flourished a V-sign in reply. If it wasn't a nautical near-miss, then it was close, and my little craft plunged and rocked alarmingly as the tanker's wake crashed into us.

There was one moment of drama which did cause me considerable alarm; my in-laws were visiting us and it had been suggested that we take a trip out to sea, not without some misgivings on my part; the group was large and my boat small. As we cleared the shore and made for deep water, hoping to see dolphins, my nose detected the unmistakeable smell of petrol. I looked around cautiously. My mother-in-law, squashed into the bow area, was sitting on a large plastic jerrycan full of fuel; its cap had popped off under the pressure and petrol was flowing out, straight into the bilge. Then, horror of horrors, I saw my mother-in-law had a glowing cigarette in the palm of her hand. An instant vision of a ball of fire flashed through my mind. Firmly, I told her to dump the cigarette overboard immediately. She did so without question. My wife looked at me quizzically. Safely ashore, I told her the reason. No further mention was made of it.

Salem himself, coming from a seafaring family, took a close interest in the 'voyages of Sindbad', as he termed them, always ready with tidal tips and advice. His father in his time had been a noted nakhoda, or skipper, plying the great dhow trade routes from the Gulf down to Mombasa and Zanzibar to bring back cargoes of rice, spices, and the mangrove poles essential for providing the roofing on treeless Bahrain. He had no modern instruments and followed a course set by the stars. When he went blind, he continued to voyage, navigating, as Salem said, by sniffing the wind off the land: 'We're off Ras Al-Khaimah now . . . we're hitting a swell, that means we're approaching the Straits of Hormuz . . . shorten sail, I can feel a squall coming on . . . ' For protection, fortunately never needed, he carried in his skipper's studded teak chest a Mauser automatic pistol which, with the wooden holster extended, became a short but lethal carbine. Thousands were sold by Germany's enterprising arms salesmen throughout the Gulf and Saudi Arabia in an early forerunner of the arms race as the twentieth century dawned.

I also took up riding again, having enjoyed it greatly during our time in Kenya, and once or twice a week, in the early evening, would take one of the thoroughbreds from the Ruler's stable out into the desert. I never flattered myself that I was a good rider, but I did know how to stay on, and I did know how to apply the brakes on an Arab horse, a skill that cannot be overvalued. I never came to grief, though one of the stallions, on my regular hacks, realising I was a novice, used to try to crack my knee against the concrete buttresses that supported a country wall, to show me who was really boss.

The family decided we needed a pet. My wife had set her heart on a saluki, the fabled hunting dog of Bahrain bred in the kennels of the Ruler and greatly prized in Saudi Arabia for its ability to run down the desert gazelle. Diffidently, I put in my request to Sheikh Isa bin Mohammed, the young member of the Ruling Family in charge of information. A fortnight later I had my answer. 'A litter has just been born,' he said. 'You're welcome to have one, but you'll have to wait four weeks.'

My children counted the days. Then at my usual weekly meeting with Isa, he told me that my puppy was ready to be collected. I asked how I was to take delivery. 'Just turn up at the palace on Sunday morning,' he told me airily. 'Behind it, you'll see a large courtyard. They're expecting you.'

With everything ready at home, puppy food stockpiled, a basket on the floor, collar and lead newly purchased, I drove up to Rifa'a. I found the courtyard as directed, parked, and walked under the archway. Any thoughts I might have had of being proudly presented with a beribboned pup evaporated as I saw a pile of russet-brown bodies in the centre, crawling over each other, yelping and fighting. The smell of dogshit was overpowering. A retainer in a dirty robe approached. I tried to explain in a mixture of Arabic and English that I was here to collect a puppy; he seemed to know all about it. He gestured to the writhing mound of salukis. 'Which is mine?' I asked. Take your pick, he indicated.

Uncertainly, I walked with him across the sand to the pack. Suddenly, they were off, scattering in all directions at our approach, then racing dementedly round the courtyard walls like frenzied competitors at a greyhound track. They passed us in a blur; the retainer grabbed one, it broke away, then another; that too escaped. Finally he pinned one up against the wall with his sandalled foot as it streaked past, grunting as it turned and bit his ankle, drawing blood. Breathless, he handed the squirming bundle of red fur over to me. I squeezed it through the barely open car door with the greatest of care and bore it home.

Shemal – we named the pup after the famous winter wind that roars through Bahrain – was, alas, initially a disappointment. He was beautiful, highly excitable, and completely wild. Naturally, house training was unknown to him, and he was covered with fleas and ticks. These I set about removing, using tweezers to pluck them from between his claws. But we grew to love him, though the children rapidly learnt to place their bare feet very carefully on the house's tiled floor during his early days. And in due course Shemal, who lived up to his name by tearing through the house like a whirlwind, settled down to a slightly more structured existence that included hitherto unknown tender loving care. Outings to the desert took on an added fascination for the family as Shemal would vanish into the middle distance, reappearing when he felt like it. Occasionally I would glimpse, in the shimmering far distance, the flowing, bounding forms of the rare wild gazelle that lived in the bare, featureless south of the island, and hold my breath, but the inexperienced Shemal never spotted them. Just as well; an armed guard patrolled the desert, tasked as their protector; he had shot at least one privately-owned saluki after it outran, then pulled down and killed one of the herd.

And if there was any time at all left on my precious Sundays, Christine and I might opt to go out for a quiet dinner. We had joined the British Club, at the suggestion of Izzard. The menu, of typically English fare, was usually first class, an improvement on some of the members. 'Just the place to pick up stories,' Ralph assured me. 'I know the club secretary. I'll set up a meeting.' He and I arrived on the appointed day, the secretary cast his eye over me and seemed satisfied. I wrote out a cheque and the matter was settled. 'I take it you're a member?' I asked Ralph. 'My dear chap,' he said, 'I wouldn't dream of it. On my first visit, as I was being interviewed by a committee member, there was a fistfight going on at the other end of the bar. The secretary turned to me and said, "Of course, you realise you'll have to serve a probationary period. We can't be too careful".'

CHAPTER FIFTEEN

What made life in Bahrain's expatriate community interesting were the larger-than-life characters. Peter Parr, the bustling, portly husband of my secretary, was one. This stalwart of the British Club had after an eventful life found a safe anchorage as an economics lecturer at the local technical college. Peter, related to the Pilkington glass family of St Helens, in England, had served in the army, finally taking to the road as an unlikely salesman after putting his end-of-service gratuity to good use in his bars of choice. He later joined the Iraq Petroleum Company, where he experienced the tragedy of losing his first wife in a flash flood as they crossed a dried-up desert water course during a weekend outing.

He was fond of relating one of the high points of his career in Bahrain's amateur dramatics, when he acted in a production of *Treasure Island*. This was recounted to Christine and myself when he visited her in hospital, recovering from a minor operation. Drink had clearly been taken prior to his arrival and he declaimed the words of Squire Trelawney in a booming voice, at the end of one scene: 'We'll find that treasure if it takes a year . . . And Hawkins (he paused for dramatic effect), Hawkins . . . shall go with us! Curtain!' And he sprang up, seized the bedside drapes and dramatically swished them across. They fell on the floor of the ward with a crash, to the amazement of passing nurses. And as an encore, he recalled a one-liner which always, in his words, brought the house down for the largely British forces in the audience: 'There's a little lugger down by Kit's Hole . . . ' It was hard to guess whether this had been a serious production or panto.

Peter was a bustling, busy little man with a shock of white hair though only forty-seven, and despite his exuberant lifestyle, was sometimes a little pompous. At a cocktail party soon after my arrival on the island, he came over. 'Andrew, I'd like to introduce you to my principal.' He turned to a tall man with a very distinctive Geordie accent. 'Meet Ernie, the head of the Gulf Technical College.' Ernie, solidly built and with a face like a crumpled tin can, was friendly and personable. Peter soon left us. 'Ah Peter,' Ernie said, 'splendid chap.' He lowered his voice. 'But a terrible piss artist.' When I rejoined Peter, pretty much the same thing happened. 'Glad you liked my principal,' he told me. He looked around, then said confidentially: 'Of course, he drinks far too much.'

The jolly German boss of a brick-laying firm from Munich threw a party to celebrate the finish of one of the immense kilns at the aluminium smelter, which he and his crew had worked on for months, laying tens of thousands of fire bricks. He imported a German oompah band, complete with lederhosen, and as it struck up the large steins of beer were passed around. The beaming Bavarian, his command of English limited and gleaned largely from the Britishers who worked with him, leaned across his wife and said conversationally to Christine, as the band pooped and parped: 'Good for the fucking, ja?'

Visitors ranged from the commonplace to the rare, even the exotic, like the gifted and undeniably different David Fanshawe, wandering composer and eccentric. This distant relative of Belgrave, whose recent choral work *African Sanctus* had won acclaim, was visiting Bahrain to record traditional songs. Wearing his trademark floppy peaked cap and carrying a tape-recorder and a little drum, his long loping figure could be seen in local villages, squatting in the dust and surrounded by crowds of excited children dancing as he pounded on his mini-bongo, returning excited at the end of each day to edit what he had gleaned.

He was to add the chants of Bahrain's pearl divers and in time

Ralph Izzard, doyen of foreign correspondents, at his Bahrain home

The Ruler of Bahrain, Sheikh Isa Al-Khalifa, at the aluminium smelter.
The author can be seen, top left

Photograph: Abdulla Khan

The Heir Apparent, Sheikh Hamed, today the King of Bahrain, demonstrates his horsemanship

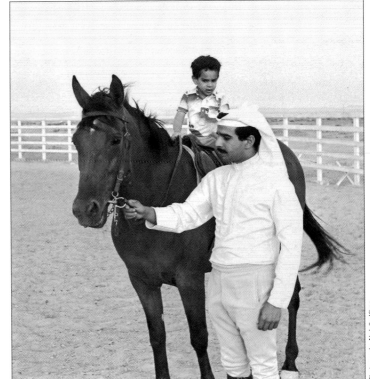

Photograph: Abdulla Khan

Sheikh Hamed with his son Sulman, today the King and Heir Apparent

The Prime Minister, Sheikh Khalifa, one of the *Gulf Mirror*'s allies
and the man who has steered Bahrain to prosperity

The author helps make
camp in the desert
during a falconry trip

The author with his
favourite pure-bred Arab
after riding in the desert

Ralph Izzard in his old Persian house with the author's daughters, Leona, left, and Sarah

Christine, the author's wife, with daughters Sarah, left, and Leona at a wedding in Bahrain

Christine, the author's wife, at a reception in Manama

The author conducts an interview with a local head teacher

The aluminium smelter had a fascination for Japanese visitors, seen with the author

The author and his wife with Salem Al-Absy, later Bahrain's ambassador to Jordan

Publication day for the author, as editor of the *Gulf Mirror*

this collection of sounds, songs and rhythms helped make up his work *Arabian Fantasy*, symphonic variations on an Arabian theme. Fanshawe, a dusty, flamboyant figure, was to continue his musical travels across the world and to achieve no small measure of fame as an almost alternative composer. He had a disregard for hardship and was tireless in pursuing his musical vision. I always appreciate a character and I found him fascinating and slightly bizarre. It was during this visit that he met and became engaged to his first wife, Judith, a secretary at the British Residency in Bahrain. The recordings he made became a symphony of the Arabian Gulf, a cantata for voices and pre-recorded tapes echoing traditional music of the Gulf.

In Europe, there was a widely-held misconception about alcohol and the Gulf. Bahrain was very decidedly 'wet'; in other states, alcohol ranged from being available quietly, under the counter so to speak, or in a quantity controlled by a liquor licence, or emphatically not all, as in Saudi Arabia. Supplies in Bahrain were effectively limitless: there were two outlets, both operated by British-controlled companies, African & Eastern, and Gray, Mackenzie. Inside, cases of beer from pretty much anywhere were stocked to the ceiling; bottles of scotch, gin and just about anything else lined the shelves. You paid your money and you made your choice. There was one qualification only: you had to be European.

In Dubai, each western expatriate was issued with a licence, with a monthly quantity sufficient for most hardened drinkers. If you wanted more, say, for a party, you had to apply to the chief of police, Jack Briggs, for a dispensation, almost always granted. In Qatar, thirsty travellers would be directed to the newly-built Gulf Hotel, which had no public bar. But it did have a special room on the fifth floor. After a soft tap, the door would swing open, bringing with it a waft of all things alcohol, but mostly beer. There, you could drink to your heart's content. For western residents in Qatar, legal supplies of alcohol were available, but discreetly.

In Bahrain, despite restrictions, locals seemed to have no difficulty in securing their own supplies. A taxi driver who picked me up at the airport asked: 'Tell me sir, do you drink?' I said I did. 'I used to,' he confided. 'I drank a bottle of whisky a day. It didn't matter what time of the day I stopped working, I would then drink a bottle of whisky, whether mid-afternoon, evening or even early in the morning. After 20 years, I decided it was a complete waste of money. I've never touched a drop since.'

As the Gulf developed, foreign lawyers found a footing. One of the pioneers was the firm of Ballantine and Miller. Bill Ballantine was a large ex-bomber pilot and his partner, Brian Miller, had been a rear gunner. It was uncharted territory for them. 'We had no idea what to charge,' said Miller, who also became a judge in Dubai. The first client was a major European oil company. 'We thought of the largest possible figure and presented our bill. To our astonishment, they paid it. And we were off – that set the benchmark.'

One London lawyer, who found highly lucrative employment further down the Gulf, in Dubai, proved a constant source of stories and tip-offs. But even for a professional of his calibre, things could occasionally go wrong for his client. He had been representing an American on some relatively trivial charge and had constantly reassured him that the matter would be dealt with summarily and he could expect nothing more than a small fine. To his amazement, his client was jailed for a year.

The prison was in the desert, rows of huts behind barbed wire, on raised land, and very definitely open air. When the lawyer finally saw his client again, he apologised profusely. 'Don't worry,' the American told him airily. 'It really isn't all that bad.' 'But what about the heat?' asked the lawyer. 'Hardly notice it, we get quite a nice breeze throughout the day.' 'The food must be awful,' the lawyer persisted. 'Surprisingly, it's really quite good. I've no complaints.' 'The warders must at least be quite brutal.' 'Not at all, it's really quite gentlemanly, the officer in charge comes round every morning to greet us and shake us by the hand.

All very civilised – except that you're still in jail at the end of it. Please don't feel bad.'

The lawyer – after all, he wasn't the one who had to go to prison – thereafter managed to live with his conscience a little easier. It is always said that doctors bury their mistakes; lawyers simply visit theirs in jail.

Another newcomer, a stout, old-fashioned veteran of the London Inns of Court, complained to me about the lack of, to him, professional standards. 'I received a call from a young fellow lawyer who wanted to see me,' he bemoaned. 'It's etiquette that, as I'm the senior lawyer, he should come to me but, oh no, I had to call on him.' He duly turned up at his colleague's law practice and waited expectantly. 'I believe we may have something in common,' the younger man, all button-down shirt and pinstripe suit, confided in him. Thoughts of the Rotary Club or even Freemasonry in the old country passed through the older man's mind. The other leaned forward. 'In England I was secretary of the Gay Liberation Front,' he said conspiratorially. Cue exit for one extremely taken aback old-style lawyer.

Then there was the eager young bank worker from the Midlands, very keen to get on, whose enthusiasm was noticed and he was posted to an outpost of the British Bank of the Middle East in Fujairah, in the southern Gulf, where he languished, lonely and depressed in this isolated banking backwater. After some months, his nerve cracked. To brighten up his day, he sent a telex to his head office in Bahrain. 'Am being sued for dereliction of duty by a local merchant,' it read. 'Intend to plead insanity.' It burst in head office like a hand grenade. His boss was on to him via the poor telephone connection within minutes. 'Oh, it was just a joke,' explained the hapless lad. He was brought back to Bahrain within days, with a black mark over his career which no doubt took years to expunge.

Johnny ffrench was the evening pianist at the airport restaurant, nervous and sensitive, a lonely soul. His father had been a high-ranking policeman in India and Johnny was sent away to England as a very little boy. He never saw his parents for years and holidays were spent alone at school, with only nuns for company – but there was a piano. And so, self-taught, he learned to play. And whenever Christine arrived for a meal, he would launch into the signature tune he had given her, *Lara's Theme* from the film *Doctor Zhivago*, because he said her high cheekbones reminded him of Julie Christie, who starred in the film.

The rumbustious Keith Lacey was a bird of a different feather, an extrovert and high-camp restaurateur whose idiosyncratic menu was nonetheless popular and he prospered, while fighting off regular attempts by his landlord to raise the rent on the little Arab house that housed his bijou eaterie. And as Bahrain thrived, so did this Channel Islander who left behind landscape gardening to follow his dream of making a living from cooking. Menus depended on what was available and the state of his finances, and were never written down. Keith would stop at each table, pose hand on hip, and launch into his repertoire for the evening. 'Well, we have our garlic beans . . . ' right through to his old standby of fondus, while backstage his assortment of friends who formed the skeleton staff struggled to heat up the cooking oil for the tiny little spirit-powered burners. Dining chez Keith was always an experience, if not particularly cheap.

Other dramatis personae included the Irish Roman Catholic priest who always wore a heavy full-length habit, with a cord round his rotund middle, even at the height of summer. Father Paddy, fat and humorous, was also a keen amateur archaeologist and was known for his large and possibly illegal collection of artefacts.

Clem Meharg, at one time the only European dentist, ran his practice from a crumbling, rundown house. Meharg, overweight and with a rich Ulster brogue, had fingers the size of bananas and was popularly supposed to be able to get them all into a patient's mouth simultaneously. Like all expatriates, he was there for the money, and life in Bahrain could be decidedly more peaceful at that time than in Belfast. 'I've been speaking to my partner back at home,' he told me as he prepared a filling. 'He'd just finished an extensive course of treatment on a patient when two gunmen burst through the door and shot him dead in the chair.' As if that wasn't bad enough, Meharg added: 'He hadn't even paid his bill' – seemingly the ultimate crime.

The British penchant for settling a person's hash was demonstrated to good effect in Bahrain. The British Club was steered by a committee of, for the most part, nondescript individuals who tended to take their role with a self-important seriousness. A new manager was appointed, a professional with a proven track record. His tenure, marked by vastly-improved menus and a professional hands-on approach to all aspects of the club, proved short-lived. He fell foul of the Great and Good. The carping and interference proved too much and he packed his bags. The primary school for expatriate children, St Christopher's, was run by the ebullient and dynamic Jimmy Adler, a Lancastrian whose bustling approach put his pupils well ahead of schools back in Britain. But after some years the school's amateur board began to find fault and cited their dissatisfaction with matters administrative. Jimmy was much admired and universally loved by his pupils. He was a good man but – as good men go – he went. A sad loss, not just for the school but for the newspaper. Jimmy had been a staunch ally.

The stream of regular visitors to Bahrain included the constant rotation of personnel for the BOAC airline, as British Airways was then known, passing to and fro on the Far East routes. First they stayed at the airline's own quarters, the down-at-heel, colonial-style Speedbird House, before being accommodated in comparative luxury at the Gulf Hotel. One of the visiting captains of the long-range VC10s was Dennis Briggs, tall and bearded, who achieved lasting fame as an RAF pilot in Coastal Command. Flying a Catalina from Northern Ireland in 1941, as part of the great

Atlantic hunt for the Bismarck, he spotted the mighty German pocket battleship, slowed down by torpedo hits from aged British Swordfish biplanes, as she lumbered along at 16 knots, making for the French port of St Nazaire and safety.

As the clouds cleared and with flak bursting all around his aircraft, Briggs told me how he managed to get off a vital sighting report as he took violent evasive action, diving and corkscrewing. The pursuing Force H of the Royal Navy, low on fuel but knowing it was vital to intercept Bismarck before she could come under air cover from the Luftwaffe, finally caught up and sank her, avenging the dramatic destruction of the battleship HMS Hood, pride of the British fleet, only days earlier, when a plunging shell from Bismarck penetrated a magazine and she blew up with only three survivors. For the rest of his life the affable six-footer was always known as 'Bismarck Briggs'.

Alan Bodger, an RAF pilot in Bomber Command during the war, also survived his turbulent time at the controls of Gulf Aviation – the airline later changed its name to Gulf Air, impressed by the abbreviation thought up by the *Gulf Mirror* – piloting it from propeller-driven aircraft into the jet age, from DC-3s to the turbo-prop Fokker Friendships, then to BAC One-Elevens and on to the majestic four-engined VC10s, before stepping up again to wide-bodied super jets. Always wearing dark glasses and chain-smoking cheroots at his desk, wreathed in clouds of smoke, he somehow managed to keep the airline airborne as he navigated round obstacles that included difficult local directors. A divorcee, he had a willowy attractive daughter, Vanessa, who scored a first for Bahrain when she opened a flower shop in the Gulf Hotel, flying in blooms from all over the world.

Hazards were something he was used to; as a wartime pilot he had undergone the horrific experience of being bombed in mid-air, flying into the path of a stick of bombs dropped by another RAF aircraft unseen above. As the flames took hold, Alan told his crew to prepare to bale out. 'Try putting her in a dive, to see if the slipstream blows out the flames,' his flight engineer urged. Alan did, it worked, the fires were extinguished and they all lived to fight another day. After going through that, the steady petty flak he had to face in the day job he could handle.

Perhaps as a result of such a high-risk life, Alan was more than usually superstitious and told me he never took any serious decision without consulting the *Gulf Mirror*'s horoscope (he never realised it was supplied weeks in advance) and once rang me in indignation to say the current one was the same as in the previous week's issue. I placated him with some talk of technical difficulties and told him brightly: 'Just consider that you've had the same amount of good luck twice.' He was unconvinced.

There was Jean Thuillier, ebullient bon viveur and former master chef who was the airline's catering chief, as demand for uplift meals grew from hundreds to thousands a week. Jean supplied a highly professional cookery column for us each week; on his annual leave, he sent back culinary reports from all over the world in his 'Travels with Thuillier' series. We never paid him anything. The phrase 'doesn't suffer fools gladly' could have been invented for the waspish Thuillier. I arrived for one of his Boxing Day dinner parties with Christine, who was wearing an uncharacteristically over-frilly dress. Thuillier, already well oiled by this time, glared at this creation. He turned to us: 'And I suppose the British ambassador's coming as a fucking Christmas tree!' You couldn't help loving him.

It was to Thuillier that I owed my growing interest in wine. As an expert, he steered my untutored palate through a host of great names, French and others, patiently explaining how best to savour them, and what separated a great Bordeaux from the also-rans. It was an education that has stood me in good stead. And then there were the Havana cigars. Again, he tutored me in exactly how to cut them and how to light them, holding the match one and a half inches above and moving the end of the cigar in a circular fashion until it was fully lit. 'You're holding the refinement of the maker's art,' he would say. 'Show it respect.' So taken was I with this that I taught my young daughters, and they would delight in lighting up a Montecristo for me, taking turns, with a long match, never, ever, a lighter. Even in these little things, Jean was a perfectionist.

It was tuition in high living from a very prince of epicurism, Thuillier's own master class for novitiates. He introduced me to Iranian caviar – the real stuff, from the Caspian Sea, the glistening, tiny grey-black eggs from the sturgeon almost worth their weight in gold. There was the rich, unique flavour of Beluga, the strong-tasting Sevruga, but both a vin ordinaire when compared to the golden 'Imperial' variety once reserved for royalty. And I was also very firmly instructed on the right way to open a bottle of champagne: not with a bang but with a whimper, letting the gas escape silently under a napkin before pouring. 'Only oiks let the cork go with a pop,' Thuillier would say disapprovingly.

While Thuillier was the cross Bodger had to bear, he couldn't say he hadn't been warned. After he had recruited the Channel Islander in London, before he returned to Bahrain he received a call from the secretary of the gentlemen's club from which Jean had just resigned. They met for lunch. 'Look, Captain Bodger,' began the little man, who incongruously wore carpet slippers in the very exclusive dining room, 'I know Thuillier is joining you. I just thought I had better warn you. He's a bit of a maverick and I've had no end of trouble with him.' 'Oh,' said Bodger, 'just what exactly do you mean?' Then followed a litany of Jean's alleged transgressions. If this was a gypsy's warning, then Bodger decided to ignore it. He may well have had cause to reflect on this in the years that followed.

Thuillier in full flow was a force to be reckoned with. He could seem unstoppable. Only once did I see him lost for words. It was something his quiet and calm wife Mary said. The occasion was a typical Thuillier big dinner party, with conversation in full and noisy flow as the cognac went round (always Courvoisier for Jean).

The topic was the sexual proclivities of one or another of fellow expatriates. Thuillier was holding forth, very opinionatedly, about the disgraceful exploits of a well-known philanderer. During a lull, Mary murmured unthinkingly: 'Well, as least he gets an erection.' You could have heard a pin drop. Her husband was dumbstruck. At last, someone changed the subject. Never underestimate the power of a woman.

But all things do come to an end. Gulf Air, in pace with its rapid expansion in the air, built a five-star hotel in Doha, capital of the neighbouring state of Qatar. It had always been Thuillier's ambition to run a modern hotel, but he was pipped at the post, and the job went to a newcomer. Then the airline commissioned an even grander hotel in Muscat. He lobbied hard for this with Bodger, refusing to take no for an answer. Finally, Bodger caved in. He told me later: 'I'm giving him this job totally against my better judgment. I've told him: the very first slip will be your last.'

Exit Thuillier, down to Muscat, and at first all went swimmingly; his organisational skills and catering knowledge served him well. Business boomed and the airline's directors congratulated themselves. But it couldn't last. Alas, once again, Thuillier over-imbibed one evening and walked into the dining room flushed and truculent. His gaze fell on an Omani guest; there was an altercation, and the angry victim was exposed to a blustering Thuillier in full flow – and in full view and hearing of other guests. Once again, Thuillier had miscalculated. The Omani was a cabinet minister. The storm broke. Twenty-four hours later, Thuillier was gone, on a one-way ticket. He and Mary returned to England, back to her home city of Sheffield, where they eventually opened a little boutique, l'elegance – the name all in lower case, of course, Jean was great for style – selling objets d'art, what else for a Channel Islander?

And Bodger? The airline boss, long single, eventually settled down with an American girl half his age, Christie Sills. Together, after he finally parted company with Gulf Air, they went to Fiji where for three years he nursed the tiny airline there into maturity before returning, and retiring, in the United States.

Major Gerald Green, the Ruler's personal aide and secretary and an incorrigible gossip about the expatriate community, was tiny, dapper and immaculately dressed in Savile Row suits; when we met at the Ruler's majlis, we would sit together and he would comment waspishly as each latecomer made an entrance. Because of his acid tongue he wasn't popular with the island's Britons; he didn't care, and why should he?

Ian Henderson, the head of the Special Branch, was the closest Bahrain had to a real hero. The Kenya-born policeman, son of a Scottish settler there, had won the George Medal for hunting down one of the leading terrorists during the Mau Mau Emergency in the early 1950s, handpicked for his fluent Kikuyu and bushcraft. Heavily disguised and with his hair caked in mud, to pass for a fugitive himself, he spent days at a time in the forest, far from help if he was suddenly ambushed, following the trail that would eventually lead him to Dedan Kimathi. Working at home late into the night, he wrote down the story of the hunt, and it was typed up by his petite fair-haired wife Marie, the love of his life, whom he had met and married in Kenya. *The Hunt for Kimathi* was published in *John Bull* magazine, earning them what at the time was a substantial sum. 'When the magazine made their offer I was staggered how large it was,' Henderson told me. 'And I thought it was in Kenya shillings, but it was British pounds, twenty times as much.' He used it to buy a car for Marie. His account went on to be published in book form, and later in paperback, and remains a collector's item.

As a child, he would go on lonely hunting safaris, accompanied only by a servant. 'He carried the rifle,' Henderson told me. 'It was too heavy for me.' Life was hard, and made harder by a Scandinavian neighbour who had agreed to let Henderson Senior water his precious herd of pedigree cattle on his land when their own bore holes dried up. When Henderson Senior came to round them up, he found they were gone – and so had the neighbour. He had sold them, loaded them up at the railhead, and vanished.

Henderson's job in Bahrain was to keep track of troublemakers and political dissidents, and run hard-core criminals to earth. His wife Marie was his personal assistant; once, when hunting the murderers who had shot dead the editor of a fledgling government newspaper, it was she who spotted the vital car clue that led them to the killers. Henderson and his team of Britons, mostly ex-Kenya police, were intelligence experts who spoke little Arabic. Their job was to investigate, following the trail and piecing together the clues, then handing over to Bahraini officers. It was they who made the arrests and carried out the interrogations.

Sitting in the Ruler's majlis, Henderson gave me a chilling insight into Sheikh Isa's character. There had been a notorious recent murder; an Omani had killed a Bahraini and he had been sentenced to death. The Sultan of Oman issued a personal plea for clemency and his letter was handed to the Ruler. In protecting the wellbeing of his own people, he was single-minded. 'He scribbled across the note, "Kill him",' Henderson related. The murderer died by firing squad.

Henderson was in some ways a stateless person. On the eve of Kenya's independence he had been deported, almost as Public Enemy Number One, for his coup in tracking down the murderous Kimathi, who became a national hero after he was hanged. He was British, but his home was Kenya, where he was born and bred. He moved south, visited what was then Rhodesia, now Zimbabwe, and worked for a while in South Africa, but found neither place to his liking. Throughout this enforced exile he kept in regular contact with Kenya's first president, Jomo Kenyatta, exchanging letters in Kikuyu. As a police officer, he had access to what had been the colonial grapevine, and through this learned of a job – head of Special Branch – that had come up in Bahrain. He was appointed and staffed it over the years that followed with former colleagues from the Kenya police force. Eventually, his banishment was lifted by the government in Nairobi and he was able to pay his first visit to the land of his birth in many years. In 2009 he bought a piece of land up-country in Nanyuki, the same township made famous by the Mount Kenya Safari Club, developed by the Hollywood film star William Holden, and built a house. Like an elephant, Ian Henderson at eighty-one was finally returning to the place of his birth.

The constant, indeed incessant, round of cocktail parties attended as much by Bahrainis as expatriates themselves, nightly turned up the same people; sometimes there were three successive functions to attend in one evening. Accountants, bankers, diplomats, oilmen, insurance men, executives of a host of companies, they were all there, the good, the bad and sometimes the ugly. Not to mention dishonest. The general manager of the Aluminium Bahrain smelter later relocated to Dubai to run a much larger smelter project, coupled with a water desalination plant, for the government there. In the years that followed, Ian Livingstone helped set up a cabal that drained some 50 million US dollars from Dubai Aluminium under bogus contracts. It was a bubble, and it did not burst for some years, until the ruling Al-Makhtoum family – spurred on by furious local merchants who felt they had been cut out of a share in the emirate's biggest cake – at last acted, after commissioning a sudden large-scale audit by a London firm of accountants.

The Al-Makhtoums, at the insistence of the hard-nosed and shrewd Sheikh Mohammed, today the Ruler of Dubai, then set its dogged little director of economic affairs on the case. It took Mohammed Al-Abbar years to unravel, using London lawyers and investigators to follow clues that led him across Europe and on to bank accounts in Panama. But Al-Abbar had a terrier-like persistence. Livingstone, then living in retirement in the south of England, was brought to book and paid Dubai – while, it must be said, denying liability – the massive sum of 15.5 million dollars in a settlement 'designed in effect to take the greatest proportion of his assets', Mr Justice Rix later commented, in 1998. And in the huge civil action that followed, a drama played out in the British courts, it was said that the metal sales agreement 'was a sham, dishonestly conceived between Mr Livingstone' and others, 'a cover for abstracting those sums so they find their way into the pockets of Mr Livingstone' and collaborators.

In all, those involved had to repay their share of the 50 million dollars they had taken, plus interest. It was a massive counter-coup by Dubai, after one of the biggest frauds seen in the Gulf. For this rogue expatriate, awarded a CBE in Bahrain during his time there for services to British industry, Al-Abbar had proved his Nemesis.

There was a sub-strata beneath this layer of westerners who were in every way as fascinating: their wives. For the most part they lived an idle, vacuous existence in their villas in Manama, their lives a procession of coffee mornings, lunches and mah-jong parties which all had a constant theme: gossip. Daily, reputations were shredded and unsuspecting newcomers provided a steady source of material. There was, inevitably, a pecking order, with those whose husbands had the biggest jobs queening it over the rest.

They had little to do with Bahraini wives or families, save for the occasional formal meeting with one of the sheikhas, herself heavily jewelled and wearing the latest Paris creations, something like going to see the Queen at Buckingham Palace, when again the pecking order came into full play. The poisonous barbs, subtly directed, could prove devastating to wives introduced into this circle. Particularly vitriolic was the Anglo-Indian wife of one executive. For these modern-day Medusas, it was their high-water mark in a superficial life, all too short before the tide turned and they returned home, back to obscurity.

The Bahraini wives themselves had their own get-togethers of a different hue, with much laughter, teasing and banter and never a western wife in sight. There was an exception. Christine was invited to a daytime pool party; when the male retainers had been safely excluded, off came the traditional gowns and necklaces and rings were shed until one by one, stark naked, they jumped into the water with much splashing and shrieks, round bottoms and bosoms glistening in the hot sun and one girl in particular, newly-wed, subjected to ribald comments and no small amount of breast tweaking. It was all innocent, happy and carefree, a far cry from the suburban world created by those other sad, lost ladies.

CHAPTER SIXTEEN

Diplomats in Bahrain in those early days were a little thin on the ground. As a British protectorate, it drew a stream of Foreign Office representatives, some at the start of their careers, others all too clearly at the end, arriving for a three-year tenure and with firm instructions not to disturb the status quo. The diplomat covering Bahrain affairs was known as the Agent; over him was the Resident, based in Bahrain and covering the whole Gulf. They were later replaced by individual ambassadors as successive states declared their independence and the United Arab Emirates was formed, made up of seven sheikhdoms that previously formed the Trucial States.

The Agent when I arrived was Alec Stirling, tall, angular and a little like those children's toys popular at the time, a long-legged bird hinging over to peck delicately at a simulated bowl of water. The bespectacled Alec, quiet, with a shy smile, was a little stiff – just like the bird. What he lacked in vitality was more than compensated for by his vivacious Canadian wife who had enough for two. Alec and I sat on the panel of the local Indian club for the judging of a beauty contest. He was visibly uncomfortable as the contestants filed past, all legs, gleaming black hair and dresses that sometimes left little to the imagination. We chose a winner, and she came forward for him to present her with the sash of honour. Awkwardly, he draped it round her. 'Go on, kiss her,' hissed his wife. He leant forward, just like the nodding bird, and planted a chaste kiss on her cheek. There was an aftermath. I received several anonymous letters in the days that followed, all claiming that the contest had been fixed, demanding a replay and naming the 'real' winner who had been cheated. Anonymous letters, I was to learn, were a feature of life in the Asian community.

Dinners with the various members of the British diplomatic corps, which always included high-ranking officers from all three services based in Bahrain, were formal affairs, not unlike dining in the officers' mess, and though the drink flowed, conversation was stilted and laughs in very short supply. The informal drinks sessions in the various service bars were a very different kettle of fish. Long service overseas tended to qualify the top officers for preference in the jostle for post-retirement perks. A very stiff and aloof former admiral ended up in charge of the lighthouses and navigational guides in the Gulf, a trifle incongruous but a not unpleasant way to while away one's later years in an untaxing sinecure; the same system of 'Buggins' turn' also existed in England, a much-coveted prize being that of defence correspondent for the Daily Telegraph, when a nod and a wink would send the job in the direction of a senior army officer, newly bowler-hatted, when it came vacant.

The British diplomat in Muscat was much warmer, good-humoured, friendly and an accomplished Arabist and historian, who had just published a book on the Trucial States, as they then were, and Oman. This book was comprehensively rubbished by Belgrave, himself an Arabist, when he reviewed it in the pages of the Gulf Mirror. Some weeks later, on the first trip I made to the magical, still almost medieval Muscat, its harbour dominated by twin forts and the city ringed by watchtowers perched on low mountain peaks, I sat with Belgrave as we met the newly-published author in his office. The pleasantries over, whiskies were served and he hesitantly brought up the subject of his book and its rough handling in my august organ. 'Er, I didn't agree completely with what had been written,' he said. 'I would be curious to know who your reviewer was.' Belgrave coughed, shuffled his feet and stared at the floor. His fate was in my hands. 'I couldn't possibly reveal that,' I said. 'A question of ethics.' 'Quite so,' he said, ever the diplomat. Belgrave was glad to escape. Had I known what a thorn in my side he was to become, I might well have acted differently.

France's man from the Quai d'Orsay, Paul Carton, based in Kuwait, was a highly accomplished performer, well selected by Paris with the aim of prising loose Britain's hold in the Gulf. In the years he travelled the region with his English wife, he was to achieve almost legendary status, unstuffy, worldly and astute. When I called on him in his office, it was nearing noon. He looked at the clock as he lit another cigarettte. 'I shall soon be posted out of the area,' he announced. 'I think we should celebrate this appropriately.' He rang a bell and a bottle of champagne on a silver tray appeared. We toasted his health, then mine, then both of us, and the bottle was empty in what seemed to be no more than ten minutes.

His range of knowledge was immense, from history, politics, and the arts through to haute cuisine, which proved useful when he later visited Bahrain. I had been given a bag of desert truffles at a village I had got to know quite well and, with guests expected within hours, we had no idea how to prepare them. I rang his hotel room. He listened as I explained our dilemma, and apologised for bothering him. He brushed aside my embarrassment. 'The honour of France is at stake,' he said. 'Au secours. Now listen carefully.' I took notes, went into the kitchen and – voila – au truffles was created by Christine. The guests seemed to like it as nothing was left.

Horses for courses. The bluff, tall Australian trade commissioner was, unsurprisingly, another bon viveur. Visits to his office usually ended with his reaching into a tiny fridge built into his gleaming mahogany desk and fishing out ice-cold tins of Swan lager. 'The sun's over the yard-arm,' he would say. 'And if it's not, then it ought to be.'

A particular friend was the Saudi charge d'affaires, Sheikh Ali, a rotund jolly bachelor who gave frequent dinner parties at his large house. Laughter and conversation always flowed easily and his eyes would light up when he recalled his previous posting to Sweden. 'Two years went like two days,' he would say sadly. Time meant nothing to this happy-go-lucky envoy. Dinner on the finest bone china, with glasses of heavy crystal, was served late into the night. I was complaining to a Bahraini minister one day that we had finally sat down to eat at 1.30 in the morning, an impossible time for most people whose working day would begin as early as 7am. 'You were lucky,' he told me. 'I was there last night and we didn't eat until 3am.'

With Bahrain's independence, diplomats were shuffled and a new breed began to appear, of a different calibre. One of the early ambassadors from Britain passed his three-year tour in a more or less permanent alcoholic haze. His eyes were glazed when he appeared at the first cocktail party of the evening, his gait unsteady an hour later, and when he arrived at the usual dinner party later he was, not to put too finer point on it, drunk. But not too drunk on one occasion to cross out his name on the place setting in front of him and pompously write on it 'His Excellency the British Ambassador', to the chagrin of the chastened hostess.

This sad representative from Whitehall would, when the annual time came to bestow the various honours allocated to him, cast them around like birdseed, reserving the highest for those who had toadied up to him when other members of the local British community had shunned him, weary of his tired and emotional behaviour. But when sober, he was a clever man, highly articulate, and for a long time the Bahrainis themselves tried to overlook this all too obvious shortcoming. By contrast, his successor was a more sober individual, dull, boring and, if he was not stupid, certainly gave every appearance of being so, which earned him the nickname 'The Dumb Ox' from mischievous Bahrainis in the government.

We saw them all, the good, the bad, the indifferent. But by contrast, in the Emirates the British ambassador, David Roberts, who was based in Abu Dhabi, was much loved, a constant help to businessmen seeking advice, and not above partaking of a large cognac as the morning's business neared its close. The afternoons were free, of course. Being a British diplomat had its compensations.

As arm's-length diplomatic relations were established with Baghdad, embassies were opened in both countries, the one in Manama guarded day and night by armed Bahraini police, not so much to keep people away but to keep close tabs on those inside. An official visit was paid to Iraq by Bahrain's Foreign Minister; I questioned this at one of my regular meetings with the Ruler. His eyes opened wide. 'Better that he should go than they should come,' he spluttered. Iraq, feared and respected throughout the Gulf, was led by a family cabal. 'They're all from the same area around a little village called Takrit,' the Special Branch's head, Ian Henderson, explained to me. That was where it all began and where it would end, years later, when Iraq's president for life, the murderous Saddam Hussein, after clawing his way over relatives to the top, was finally hunted down by soldiers of the U.S.-led invasion force and captured where he had literally gone to earth, like a cornered fox, in a roughly dug hiding place. He was to share the fate of his countless victims, by hanging, in a semi-public execution, defiant to the end.

Internationally, as far as the world's press was concerned, Bahrain was not really on the map and the visiting firemen, as we called them, would take a swing down the Gulf at irregular intervals, sometimes from their Beirut base but more usually from further afield. The Reuters man was the most in evidence among these birds of passage and was able to sell their news service to government ministries in most of the states. Eventually Reuters took the plunge and established a permanent correspondent in Bahrain.

Enter Colin Fox, 6ft 5in and skinny with it, cool, calm and professional, a newsman's newsman, with his stunning Danish wife Marianne. Colin quickly won the confidence of Bahrain's

Ministry of Information and also established himself as a Jack of all trades for his office. If his wire link went down, he would be seen, screwdriver in hand, delving inside his teleprinters; if anything broke, Colin was always on hand to fix it. In his leisure time he drove round the island at high speed in his white Peugeot, a cloud of dust trailing behind him. The couple's hospitality was famous – Marianne was an accomplished chef, and any evening in their lofty apartment overlooking the Gulf always ended with repeated libations of Colin's favourite tipple, the peaty Islay malt whisky Laphroaig.

But Colin was also intrepid, at times almost reckless. Some years into his stay in Bahrain, he and Marianne were driving in the desert south of the island when he saw a drill rig in the distance, enveloped in a white cloud. His curiosity aroused, he drove over, leaving the car a distance away. He mounted the steps; the rig was deserted and the noise deafening. The cloud was in fact escaping gas. The rig had suffered a major blow-out, the crew had fled and there was Colin, by now on the second storey and beginning to realise that perhaps he shouldn't be there. Even the friction of a nylon shirt is enough under those circumstances to produce a spark of static electricity. It had been a close call.

Bahrain had proved a home from home for the Foxes and their two children; when they left, the Ruler presented them with a canteen of silver cutlery. His next posting was nothing like as enjoyable: to West Africa, where Colin soon found himself in a hot, sweaty prison cell after his objective reporting had provoked a government official. He was sprung by Marianne, who was able to enlist the French ambassador on their behalf. They were a formidable team.

Not all journalists behaved themselves. A reporter from one of Britain's leading quality Sundays spent a week on the island, gathering material for one of the tedious supplements that seemed to be published almost every week, their heavy advertising content proving highly profitable. On his last night, this particular journalist was invited to the large home of the head of a major British company. The room was filled with the usual familiar faces on the cocktail party circuit and this pompous and not a little self-important scribe drank deep at the well of hospitality. Too deep. Seeking the nearest cloakroom, he stumbled into the bedroom of his host and hostess, all garish carpet, large bed and various lavish drapes, where he projectile-vomited across the room. There was a shriek from his hostess when it was discovered but by that time he was away, stumbling off into the night where he was never seen or heard of again – in Bahrain.

The *Daily Mail*'s waspish writer Ann Leslie stopped off as part of a Middle East tour and later wrote scathingly of the expatriate community, in a general piece about Bahrain. Ann, one of Fleet Street's leading commentators, was never one to suffer fools gladly and in Bahrain found her patience sorely tried. She found little to detain her and her visit was brief.

One day a hesitant, polite little man walked into my office. He introduced himself as the *Frankfurter Allgemeine Zeitung*'s represent-ative: Baron von Munchausen. Yes, you couldn't make it up. 'I've spent the greater part of my life trying to live it down,' he said. Unlike the tall stories attributed to his famous ancestor, the baron provided somewhat more accurate coverage. He insisted on meeting Ralph, whose reputation still lived on among the press corps in Germany, and Ralph was happy to provide a supply of ice-cold Tuborg lagers after I drove the good baron round to his little oasis home.

Ralph turned the tables neatly on a New York correspondent who had been billeted on him. This man was impossibly boring, very trying for Ralph, and this was made worse by his guest lecturing the veteran journalist on how stories should really be covered. The visitor returned one lunchtime from a meeting with the Foreign Minister in a state of excitement. 'I've got an exclusive,' he told Ralph. 'This is how it should be done.' He laboriously wrote it out, then proudly showed it to Ralph. 'When do you plan to file?'

asked Ralph. 'In a couple of hours, no rush, there's a lengthy time difference. I'll walk over to the wire office this afternoon.' He retired to his room for a well-earned siesta. Ralph immediately phoned the story through to the *Financial Times* in London as his guest snored; it received exclusive billing. The visitor never suspected. It really was true what is said about the newspaper business: great journalists are born, not made.

One of the biggest stories covered by the *Gulf Mirror* – and by the world's press – was also one of the most dramatic: the day the Bapco refinery caught fire. A storage tank, long overdue for maintenance, suddenly ruptured. More than 12,000 barrels of base stock for jet fuel flowed out of Tank 474 down into trenches and then somehow ignited. Flames and thick black smoke billowed out, taking everyone by surprise. It happened on a Friday in November 1972, the weekly day of rest, and oil company workers were relaxing by playing golf, cricket, sailing or simply downing a few beers. A general alarm was sounded, for the first time ever, and expat employees, many still wearing short-sleeved shirts and shorts, were bussed in as makeshift fire-fighters.

The heat generated by the flames was also felt in the boardroom. By great ill fortune for the oil company's local management, the annual meeting of Bapco's directors was taking place, with board members having flown in from all over the world. What business they had to discuss was rendered irrelevant as they faced the prospect of seeing the very reason for their being there literally go up in smoke. At the end of these meetings the PR department in Awali would issue a carefully worded press release that told no one anything. The oil companies like to keep their business private. And in this case of imminent disaster the department's chief, a smug long-time company servant, hair slicked back, proved up to the challenge. With flames leaping at night hundreds of feet into the air, clearly visible from the roof of my home in Manama, 12 miles away, he blandly told the world's media that there was no fire.

It raged for six days, destroying seven other tanks and a power plant as burning oil overflowed from the protective bunds, which proved woefully insufficient, spilling into other tank areas and down the pipeline trenches into the refinery itself, wrecking processing units.

The fire service irregulars, struggling to direct inadequate hose-pipes to cool down tanks at risk of collapsing, at one point had to run for their lives as a huge tank burst open, sending a massive fireball roaring into the sky. They leapt fences, hurdled pipelines and jumped ditches as the flames streaked past them, causing savage burns to the backs of ears, necks, elbows and legs which took months to heal. At night, off-duty staff took a break from fighting this inferno, packing the Bapco club's bar, still high on adrenaline and excitement, many with cruel blistered burns on ears and elbows clearly visible when I interviewed them.

As the fire raged on, nerves began to crack and there were calls across the island – and even in Bapco itself – to bring in Red Adair, the legendary Texan who specialised in snuffing out well-head blazes. Bapco decided to go it alone, and fire-fighting intensified, but now with personnel wearing the proper equipment. Eventually, it burnt itself out and the oil company was left to take stock. Throughput at the refinery, which handled crude from Saudi Arabia via an undersea pipeline, as well as a much lesser amount from Bahrain's tiny oilfield, was cut by eight per cent, down to 238,000 barrels daily. And the major clean-up operation and repair work that followed held up work on building a massive desulphurisation plant to produce fuel oil for the Japanese market. The bill was high.

Then the inquest began. The results were a damning indictment of management. Tank 474, the cause of the fire, had been due for shutdown for several years; this had been put off and major corrosion went unchecked. When it eventually split, the metal was the thickness of a toothpaste tube at the point of rupture. The protecting bund – walls of earth surrounding it – was not able to contain the spillage, and the fuel flowed out and eventually ignited.

On-stream inspection did not provide sufficient coverage, the investigators ruled, and fire-fighting facilities were totally inadequate. And the root cause: Bapco's policy of maximising throughput at the expense of maintenance and inspection. Procedure manuals at the refinery and at Caltex plants through-out the world were hastily rewritten. A classic case of closing the stable door after the horse had bolted. Did heads roll? Probably; such disasters are usually laid at the door of the person least able to defend himself. But if the axe did fall, it fell a long way from Bahrain, and the management team survived. And the PR department? It continued to live up to its motto of the silent service: hear no evil and speak no evil, no matter how often others see it.

The *Gulf Mirror*, of course, put its own interpretation on the blaze, gleaning what little information I could, but there was no denying our dramatic front-page picture of flames reaching up into the night sky, taken by the redoubtable Abdulla Khan.

CHAPTER SEVENTEEN

In the early months of the newspaper I was able to forge lasting alliances with the people of Bahrain who made the news as readily as they made money. The sheikhdom's merchant princes were staggeringly rich, by any standards. Their success had brought penthouses in London, vast apartments in Manhattan, imposing seafront houses on the Riviera. Foremost among these modern-day moguls were the Kanoos, who had built up a service industry to shipping, then diversified into almost every area, from tractors to travel, with offices right through the Gulf. The group was headed by Ahmed, forthright, jovial and tough. With his no-nonsense brother Mohammed, later stricken by Parkinson's disease, he had grown the business, begun by their father, from early beginnings that had included both of them heaving mail sacks into lighters from freighters moored offshore. Mubarak, the third member of their triumvirate, kind, shrewd and jokey, operated in a different way from the others' hard-nosed approach. It was he who handled government relations, smoothed over problems, cleared the way; Mubarak was never a man to be underestimated. Then there was Abdulla, loud, burly and an agile traditional dancer at the Kanoos' weekly supper gatherings, with local musicians singing the songs of the pearl fleets; with Abdul-Aziz, Abdulla ran the Saudi office, where he was a powerful force, with strong links to the royal family.

There was Hussein Yateem, sent to England before the Second World War to learn English; as a right-hand man to Bahrain's rulers and petroleum companies, he had made himself indispensable, and prospered. His son Ali, gentle, unassuming, who always wore western dress, was one of my directors; he was always in my corner. Yousuf Al-Moayyed, the newspaper's landlord, garnered a variety of local agencies, from cars to cranes, and would proclaim himself to newcomers as 'the richest man in Bahrain'. His son Farouk, was also a director of the *Gulf Mirror* and he, too, was an ally. A fellow member of the board was Shawqi Zayani, whose family owned the Delmon Hotel. Shawqi had been steadfast in his support of me and my family, particularly over the problems with our accommodation. He arranged for us to stay at the hotel free when we needed to bridge the gap between leaving Ralph's beautiful old home and moving into our new temporary accommodation. Shawqi was a man of many parts, erudite, well read and a sharp conversationalist with a ready wit. He would tut-tut when I recounted the hurdles I had had to surmount. 'Hasad' he would murmur – the Arabic word meaning jealousy.

Mohammed Ali Al Hasan won the contract from Bapco to supply bottled gas through the island and offshore. He sold the gas cookers, and the gas to fuel them. If you were to live in Bahrain, then you met him, kindly, courteous, wise. And also a very good salesman; few people bought electric ovens after that first meeting. His thriving business could really be said to be cooking on gas.

Bahrain's mercantile tradition was almost as old as the island itself. In the early days trading was modest: dates, weaving, pottery, and of course pearls. Bahrain was a safe anchorage, and an essential halfway house for the great dhows that plied the waters of the Gulf from Kuwait in the north down to the Straits of Hormuz, then across to India and down to Mombasa and Zanzibar. In Bahrain they would trade, pick up supplies and replenish their water from the island's springs.

Commerce was a vital part of the island's life and as trade slowly expanded, so did the fortunes of those who made it their business. From the early houses built of coral blocks there grew more robust constructions; this meant shipments of cement, mangrove poles for the roofs, tiles for the flooring. As the cargos became bulkier, the need for deep-water jetties became obvious. The early modest quays of local stone were replaced by cement blocks; cranes became necessary, replacing the chains of stevedores who emptied the lighter holds sack by sack. The shopping lists grew, and the vision – or ambition – of the merchants grew with them. The tiny lock-ups were replaced first by depots, then by warehousing; from the unpretentious houses to today's marble-floored skyscrapers, everything had to be brought in by sea. It was a process of evolution that with the discovery of oil suddenly speeded up.

It was from these early beginnings that the open-fronted shops were to blossom into grandfather-to-grandson family businesses and in turn grew into dynasties; the names of Bahrain's merchants became a roll-call of a new super-merchant class: the Al-Moayyeds, the Jalals, Almudaifas, Zayanis, Shariffs, Wazans. And of all of these, the greatest were to become the Kanoos and Yateems.

Hussain Yateem, modest, softly-spoken, never flamboyant, was a dynamo, and he rose, if not from nothing, then close to it. Orphaned at twelve, he was despatched by far-sighted relatives to England to learn the language, arriving at Brighton after a lengthy voyage on a slow boat from Basra. When his uncle, who had founded the family business with Hussain's father, moved up to Kuwait, the young boy was recalled to take charge of the Bahrain operations: cement and construction equipment. A. M. Yateem Brothers also ran a store begun by his grandfather, a pearl merchant who brought back medicines from India to sell in his shop.

Hussain's English proved a vital qualification: he became an oil company translator and played a key role in negotiations with Gulf rulers. This in turn yielded a profitable spin-off: when oil was found in Bahrain, the Yateems became a major supplier for the Bahrain Petroleum Company. Standard Oil of California also needed Hussain when it hammered out deals for concessions in what were the Trucial States, now the United Arab Emirates. As the trickle of westerners coming to the Gulf swelled to a flow,

Hussain realised they would need air-conditioners and he started to import them; business expanded to include an ice and water plant, and the astute Hussein also began buying land. In 1938 he built Bahrain's first filling station, outside the Bab Al-Bahrain, the arched entrance to the old suq and, influenced by life in Britain, opened the island's first cinema. Years later the petrol station was replaced by the Yateem family with a mosque, the stark simplicity of its beautiful white-painted minaret and dome contrasting with the multi-storey office blocks around it.

Enter Freddie Bosworth in 1949, a former RAF pilot who arrived penniless but with an old war-surplus aircraft and a dream of forming a flying club. Hussain lent him his start-up capital – in those days there were no banks to borrow from. A year later Gulf Air was formed and as it expanded from prop aircraft to the two-engined BAC One-Eleven jets, then to the four-engined majestic VC10s and finally to the jumbo era of Tristars, Hussein was always in the background, sitting on the airline's board for twenty-five years. At the same time he was importing a host of consumer goods, from cars to watches, and the compound of detached villas he built on the outskirts of Manama provided luxury accommodation for overseas executives with Cable & Wireless and other companies. Yateem Gardens, heavily planted with date palms, became one of Bahrain's most desirable addresses and a key part of the family business. For Hussain himself, who also lived there, other homes included an apartment off Park Lane in London, close by the Dorchester Hotel, and a home in the south of Spain, where he would escape the mid-summer heat of Bahrain. Today the modern Yateem Centre in Manama houses more than a hundred shops and many offices.

In an earlier era, when it had been unusual for a Bahraini to venture further afield than neighbouring countries and, of course to India, Hussain had travelled widely with rulers on official visits, visiting the World Fair in New York in 1939. In the United States, he met President Roosevelt, and he was in London for the coronation of Queen Elizabeth in 1953, when he met Winston Churchill. He went on to become a philanthropist, helped found the National Bank of Bahrain, became a member of the Gulf Hotel board, and one time headed both the Chamber of Commerce and Bahrain Red Crescent Society.

Hussain Yateem was a man far sighted and wise beyond his time. He was also one of the best ambassadors Bahrain has ever had, unofficial and unpaid. Today the House of Yateem, with 650 staff, is still very much a family business with no plans to go public. Hussain's son Ali – a member of the newspaper's board and one of my staunch allies – is managing director; another son, Mohammed, is also on the board, together with daughters Mary, Salwa and Shehrazad.

The House of Kanoo, with more than 4,000 employees by 2008 and a network of offices numbering 90, may have been built on sand but its foundations were solid. Its founding father was Haji Yusuf bin Ahmed Kanoo, who set up business in 1890, but its pre-eminent position not only in the Gulf but throughout the Middle East was the result of the vision of three men: the wily, cautious Ahmed, the burly sometimes confrontational Mohammed, and the gently, kindly Mubarak. Each in his own way had a vital role to play: Ahmed, the strategist, oversaw the Kanoo blueprint for growth, expanding into a variety of agencies and displaying a flair worthy of a great financier; it was Mohammed's job to make these projects work – and he did just that, focusing on the detail (not for nothing was he nicknamed 'The Cannon' by a previous ruler, Sheikh Sulman – he was unstoppable). I once asked his advice when I had upset the British Agent, Alec Stirling, over a report in the paper. 'None of his business,' he growled. Mubarak was despatched as literally a flying entrepreneur, wooing the rulers of Abu Dhabi and Dubai in a lengthy courtship that led to permission to become established in both sheikhdoms; then followed Sharjah. His extensive journeying, earlier as a student and later for the family, led to him developing an interest in travel and in 1946 he opened the first travel agency in the Gulf, in Bahrain. Then it was just two staff using a station wagon to pick up expatriates from their homes and ferry them to the airport; today it is a sophisticated network operating through the Gulf and with offices in Europe.

The Kanoos have always been hands-on. Ahmed and Mohammed would themselves work on the barges that ferried fuel to flying boats moored offshore; they would also help unload cargos from lighters for trans-shipment. When Mubarak was sent to school in India the family could not afford a cabin so he slept on deck for the 11-day voyage to Bombay. Later, to get to Beirut, where he had enrolled at the university, he travelled by dhow to Kuwait, rode a lorry to Basra, then went by train to Baghdad and on to Damascus before the final leg to Lebanon. All three were no strangers to hardship, privation and physical hard work as they strived for their family business in those early days.

I received a call from Mubarak one day. 'I thought we were your friends,' he said sorrowfully. 'Why? What's the matter?' I asked. 'Come over and see me,' he said. In his office he was pouring over a list of names. It was the passenger manifest for a flight that had left Bahrain for London early that morning. 'Your wife and children have flown back to England,' he said, 'but they booked their tickets through Mohamed Jalal's travel agency.' I could have kicked myself. Christine had agreed to travel back with Jalal's English wife Jane, and it seemed natural to combine booking arrangements. Too late. I realised my mistake. I could only apologise. The astute Mubarak perused the British Airways passenger lists daily. The Kanoos had their regular customers and as Mubarak was now demonstrating, were not slow to protect their interests. I duly took note.

Today the legacy of those early pioneers is the great strength of a group worth billions of dollars. Like the Yateem Group, it refuses to go public and the family refuses to rely on borrowed capital. Employees are seen as a vital part of an extended family which is committed to ploughing something back into the community, endowing hospitals and clinics, and helping those less fortunate. The family were prominent in establishing Bahrain's Beit Al Qur'an, the only institute of its kind dedicated to the Qur'an and the preservation of historical holy manuscripts. It was the dream of Abdul Latif Kanoo, an engineer by training, who donated his collection of rare manuscripts, art and ceramics to the centre, conceived in the tradition of the madrassahs attached to the Middle East's great mosques.

That pioneering threesome, Ahmed, Mohammed and Mubarak, took a close interest in the *Gulf Mirror*, and indeed jointly had a shareholding. Each week when I met them, they took a personal interest in the stories we carried and helped me through any difficulties I might meet, providing a sympathetic ear but never with any pressure or interference. I forged a close relationship with the trio and Christine and I would meet them weekly at their guest house in the sprawling Kanoo compound, where local musicians with drums and the traditional oud – a stringed instrument – would sway together as they roared out songs from the pearling fleets.

Sometimes a lanky local dancer would leap into the middle of the room, twisting and gyrating, his long hair flailing. He would be joined by the agile Abdullah, later to become the overall head of the group, leaping and springing, first down on his haunches then aloft, in a display of exuberance by a natural dancer. Abdullah and his brother Abdul-Aziz, who both ran the Saudi side of the business, jewel in the crown of the Kanoo group, were also to become close friends, providing wise counsel and more than a little moral support.

Today, with younger members of the family moving up the management structure, the group has firmly embraced the computer age and continues to expand in its areas of general trading, shipping, insurance and travel, helped by a management team that includes top personnel from Europe. But its founding traditions remain as strong today as they ever were, guided by one of Arabia's proverbs: Cherish your brother, for he who is brotherless is like a warrior without weapons.

Busy though Bahrain was, I still found time for business trips down the Gulf, visiting Qatar, Abu Dhabi and Muscat, struggling to move into the current century after the overthrow of the tyrannical Sultan Bin Taimur and his replacement by his Sandhurst-trained son, Qaboos. Outside the ancient forts, makeshift car barriers were provided by rows of muzzle-loading ships' cannon from long-gone men-of-war, sunk up to the breeches in the sand. From the arsenal of one of the forts commanding the little harbour, I was shown a ship's cannon ball, still wrapped in greaseproof paper, exactly as it came from the ironfounders in London.

A senior Muscat minister was much taken with my visit, and with the *Gulf Mirror*, which circulated strongly there. He spoke of a gift. At the tiny airstrip, as I waited to leave, a gowned figure hurried in and handed me a brown paper bag. Mystified, I fumbled inside. It contained a tiny brass coffee pot, metal tassel on the spout and inlaid with silver. It stands on my fireplace to this day. When I returned to Bahrain, Jawad Al-Arrayed spotted it and asked how I had got it. I told him. 'That is one of the very few, really genuine coffee pots in the Gulf. They are impossible to find. Treasure it.' The minister himself was shot dead only weeks later, in a family squabble in Abu Dhabi.

One week an invitation dropped on to my desk for a visit with a difference. It was from the government of Abu Dhabi, requesting the *Gulf Mirror*'s presence at celebrations the following week marking national day. The usual festivities, fireworks and receptions, were planned but the highlight was a performance in a sports arena by Om Kolthoum, known throughout the Arab world as the Nightingale of the Nile. This was something that could not be missed and Abu Dhabi was paying for everything, air fare and hotel stay. The concert was on a Sunday, the day immediately after publication, and the only flight I could get was at 7am. This meant no sleep after my usual press ordeal.

I arrived in dusty Abu Dhabi in the heat of a roasting day, was met by a reception committee from the ministry of information and taken to my hotel, modest in those days of a still largely undeveloped Gulf state, but it did have a bar. Early that evening a large limousine arrived to collect me and we arrived at the stadium. Parked Mercedes cars were jam-packed in the streets outside; several, I noted, had Kalashnikovs and bandoliers of ammunition clips left casually on the rear window shelves, with no one around and no security.

Inside the stadium, the seats were packed, the air of anticipation electric. Om Kolthoum, then in her sixties, was a legend and her performances could last hours. Born in Egypt around the beginning of the twentieth century, she had been a household name in the Arab world, touring Damascus, Baghdad and Beirut. The diva, by now overweight, finally strode on to the stage, the orchestra struck up and the voice that has fascinated Maria Callas, Salvador Dali and even Bob Dylan, Led Zeppelin and Bono, began to sing.

The audience was enraptured, even mesmerised, as her magnificent contralto voice rose and fell, sometimes sobbing as she sang of love, longing and loss. Not, it must be said, to everyone's taste outside the Middle East but the audience was transfixed; this was a Middle East version of Beatle-mania. Old men with grey beards wept, threw themselves to the ground, held each other, howled out declarations of undying love and even proposals of marriage. And still the performance went on, for hours. She was said never to sing a line the same way twice, altering the emphasis and intensity to bring listeners to a state of euphoria as singer and audience fed off the other's emotional energy. The Star of the East showed no sign of exhaustion, but I did and I left long before the end, drained from lack of sleep. As a spectacle it had been unforgettable and I felt privileged. When Om Kolthoum died in 1975, her funeral in Cairo drew four million mourners and predictably ended in pandemonium.

On another visit to the Southern Gulf, it was in the neighbouring state, Dubai ,that I met the legendary Sheikh Rashid Al-Makhtoum, hawk-eyed and hook-nosed, a Bedu ruler from a traditional background presiding over a modern economic miracle. In the sand-blown emirate, the bustling waterfront gave an indication of the dynamism that would propel this tiny sheikhdom to the forefront of the Middle East. I met his secretary, a sleek, oily clerk who held the key of the door to the Ruler himself, and then, at his beachfront home, the Ruler's inscrutable and mysterious grand vizier, the billionaire Bahraini who had steered the state to its pre-eminence.

Mahdi Al-Tajir was born into a Bahraini family, and like many of the island's Shias his dark complexion betrayed a different bloodline from Sunnis. He had an elementary education, combined with an upbringing in which Islam played an overshadowing part; as a child, he was made to memorise large tracts of the Koran and, like other children from a similar background, learnt to live on his wits. But it was evident from an early age that he was bright. It was this alertness, this quickness to learn, that singled him out when he joined the customs department. His sharpness, his constant questioning of decisions, his ideas, exhausted the patience of the staid Britisher running the department, who found him too clever by half.

The young official was surrounded by wealth, the wealth of greedy merchants accustomed to circumventing irksome regulations with bribes that could range from a gold watch, a Persian carpet or a wad of notes. Then there was the wealth of the ruling family, when to have the name Al-Khalifa meant preferment, cars, a large villa, trips to Europe, first class, there to stay in the best hotels, all through the largesse of the Ruler.

This the young Al-Tajir had grown up with. Those who worked with him found he had a ready wit, and the English he had picked up, helped by lessons at school, became fluent, and he learnt to find his way through the complex labyrinth of customs rules and regulations – in English. Yet colleagues also fond something dis-turbing, an inner strength, an inscrutability. He had a penetrating stare, his hard, dark-brown eyes set in a moon face that gave nothing away.

Bahrain's customs department ran like a well-oiled machine, and like many government departments in the stable sheikhdom, was the envy of its barely-developed neighbours. The young Bahraini's chance came. His English manager, constantly irritated, at last found the opportunity to rid himself of his tiresome subordinate when Dubai requested assistance in expanding its own customs department. He nominated his unruly colleague, and the rest is history.

Al-Tajir arrived in the dusty, backward and unruly member of the Trucial States, as it was then, and set about the organisation of a customs office modelled on Bahrain's, while at the same time winning the confidence of Sheikh Rashid. He showed the combative ruler how to increase his income beyond his dreams, imposing an import tax on a thousand different goods where none has previously been levied, in return for guarantees of a thriving entrepot trade across the waters of the Gulf with the giant all the Arab states had to live with, Iran, then a spider's web of government corruption under the rule of the decadent Pahlevi dynasty of the Shah.

The young customs official was fluent in Farsi and in the space of two years had made himself a trusted servant to Rashid; trade boomed, revenues soared, with the big jets flying in several times a week from London, Paris and Rome to deposit their cargoes of gold bullion worth millions of dollars in wooden boxes on the edge of the runway; no one would dare touch them. From there they would be picked up for onward shipment by fast dhow, running the gauntlet of patrol boats to be smuggled into India. For Dubai was the centre of this thriving trade, where one trip could cover all costs: the boat, its powerful engine, and the crew's wages. All subsequent trips were virtually pure profit, in a trade totally legal in Dubai's waters but totally illegal when the consignments arrived off India. The Bahraini oversaw many of the thriving syndicates, always cutting a generous share for his master and of course himself.

But this was only to be an appetiser. The big oil companies had begun making overtures to the Gulf state. Rashid asked his young aide for his advice. And it was the Bahraini who negotiated the contracts that laid the foundation for Dubai's future as the Hong Kong of the Middle East. The confidential agreement also concealed a generous percentage for Rashid's faithful servant that was to provide him over time with riches 'beyond the dreams of avarice', as a member of the ruling family later described to me.

The wily Rashid knew, of course. But by now Al-Tajir had become indispensable. The big developers came to Dubai, project followed project; Dubai prospered in a way that would have been unimaginable only ten years previously. Rashid became rich, and his man became richer. It was said that there wasn't a major deal done in the tiny state in which the Bahraini did not have a cut. And as Rashid said, as the jealousy grew, quoting an old Arab saying, 'You don't stop the ox from eating the corn'.

The Bahraini himself, with his mixture of arrogance, truculence and insouciance, faced down his accusers, one after the other. He made no attempt to hide his wealth, living in his spacious beachside house with works of art from all over the world, and a collection of Persian carpets almost priceless. And day after day, at Rashid's majlis, or in the desert, during the frequent hunting trips to Pakistan, when the sleek falcons would be loosed to bring down the huge, lumbering bustard, he was always there, at the Ruler's side. Rashid was comfortable with his Bahraini, who possessed a constant flow of anecdotes, jokes and fables. He became in truth almost like another son.

And the Ruler's own three sons, if they felt jealous in those early days, were won over, one by one. Al-Tajir would one day be challenged and stripped of his power by the combative Sheikh

Mohammed, later to succeed his older brother Makhtoum as Ruler, but for years the Bahraini was the undisputed power behind this desert throne. He never wore a wristwatch. He had learned not to. Dozens, scores, he had given to others when they, knowing of his great wealth, asked for the one he wore. In the Arab tradition, you give to those who have not. And what was a watch?

Some said he had become a man without conscience, that he had sold his soul. Al-Tajir was always kind to me, but how was his transformation to one of the richest men in the world viewed in Bahrain, where the prodigal son had never been forgotten? I asked Mohammed Kanoo. 'Without him, Dubai would have been nothing,' he said. 'Good luck to him.'

The Bahraini went on to acquire a portfolio of property in Europe worthy of a potentate: 18,000 acres in the Scottish Highlands, a palatial London home, and a huge estate in northern France, complete with chateau, lake and forest, its mega-acreage contained by a high wall. For some years he was ambassador in London for the United Arab Emirates and his interests in metal trading, oil and gas continued to burgeon until, by the first decade of the new millennium, he was rated in the *Sunday Times* Rich List as the world's 26th wealthiest man, worth an estimated £2.2 billion. Not bad for a customs officer.

CHAPTER EIGHTEEN

Bahrain, though an independent state, had had treaty relations with Britain since 1820 and the Royal Navy operated from a large base at Jufair, complete with arsenal with concrete walls six feet thick. The RAF, with a squadron of fighters and a range of transport aircraft, was on Muharraq; the Army in a clutch of encampments, including Hamallah, out in the desert. For expatriates in Bahrain, the presence of the forces helped to lift their life, with military band concerts, constant receptions and cocktail parties; for Bahrainis, much of the forces' pay found its way into the suq. 'The British boys', as the locals called them, were generally well behaved, and it was to them that the taxi drivers owed their fluent English. Drunkenness was low-key, though there were frequently men overboard when the liberty boats ferried back crews from shore leave to warships at anchor offshore.

It was an arrangement that worked for both Bahrain and Britain: the sheikhdom reaped the harvest of British money and protection; Britain had a valuable staging post en route to the Far East. It had to end. It was a commitment that the Chiefs of Staff could no longer afford; Whitehall announced that the forces had to leave and the bases, with a range of civilian support services, all from Britain, must close.

Bahrain was wooed by local suitors; Britain's absence would leave a power vacuum that had to be filled; there were high-level talks over possible membership of the soon-to-be formed United Arab Emirates, with Kuwait, and with Qatar. Finally, the Ruler decided: Bahrain would go it alone. On Saturday, August 14, 1971, he proclaimed the Bahrain islands an independent sovereign state – very convenient for the *Gulf Mirror*, the day before publication. I managed a wrap-round front-page souvenir issue, and borrowed the official red shield, the government's crest, to display at the top of page one. The banner headline caused me some anxious moments. Then I put aside any reservations and borrowed from Aldous Huxley: Brave New Bahrain shrieked the front page. Any doubts I might have had were dispelled when I met Sheikh Mohammed bin Mubarak, the Foreign Minister, at our weekly 'morning prayers' session. 'Just brilliant,' he enthused. 'Now that's what I call journalism.' His comments cancelled out, I thought, the rebuke from the government's legal department about using the official seal. The issue was a sell-out.

Membership of the United Nations followed, and I was there in New York for the official reception, taking advantage of a free ticket from British Airways to mark the inaugural transatlantic flight of its jumbo 747 service.

I joined Sheikh Mohammed bin Mubarak and we chatted over drinks in the UN's skyscraper riverside headquarters with Sir Alec Douglas-Home, Britain's lofty Foreign Secretary and former Prime Minister, who had an air of mild bemusement as delegates jostled and pushed around him.

It was a four-day trip that I made the most of, touring Manhattan, making a special purchase at Tiffany's for my wife, and dining at 21, the famous restaurant, with Gerry Stein, son-in-law of one of the founders, who had become a good friend in Bahrain. Displayed prominently at the entrance was a large scale model of a Bahraini dhow, beautifully crafted in the finest detail, a gift from Ahmed Kanoo. 'I've got the worse middle name in the world,' Gerry confided as we ate soft-shell crabs, 21's speciality. 'No, you haven't,' I came back. 'It can't worse than mine.' 'Right,' he said, 'my middle name's Mervyn. Beat that.' I was ready. 'I can,' I said. 'Mine's Melvyn.' I think I won on points.

It was at one of Jean Thuillier's celebrated private dinners in Bahrain that I first met Gerry, whose catering firm supplied Gulf Air. Annually, he and Thuillier arranged a dinner, vying to see who could lay on the most exclusive wines. That evening, Thuillier was sure of success; his chosen bottle stood on a little table, uncorked, and with a paper serviette on top, protecting the contents. Then came the moment. Each guest received an inch in his glass; it was truly exquisite, particularly for me, whose palate was undergoing regular tuition from Thuillier, himself a proud Chevalier du Tastevin, an honour bestowed by France complete with tiny silver tasting cup.

As his guests, presidents, vice-presidents and aviation VIPs, contemplated their empty wineglasses, a huge arm descended across the tables, sending everything flying. Two hairy fingers tweaked the bottle off its stand; the next moment it was upended, into the gaping mouth of one of the airline's board members, Adel Algosaibi, from Saudi Arabia. The bottle drained, he set it down with a bang. 'Thuillier,' he boomed, 'that was excellent. Bring out another.'

A stunned Thuillier could only stutter, in disbelief, 'but sir, that is the only bottle this side of France.'

Producing the bumper independence issue laid the ground for an even more ambitious edition some weeks later: the tenth anniversary of the Ruler's accession. Preparations had gone on for months in Manama for a week of celebrations. And also for the *Gulf Mirror*; this had to be something special.

I had carefully hoarded photographs from all over the island, commissioned articles, special artwork, and established a separate section in my little office where the task of producing the supplement went on side by side with the work of producing that week's regular issue. The press overseer, Matthew, entered into the spirit with energy. Then, to set the seal on it, I obtained permission for a special commemorative portrait of the Ruler, in full colour, for a glossy front page; Abdulla Khan, our trophy photographer, made the appointment and waited while Sheikh Isa changed into his finest ceremonial robes.

Work, always a burden, went into overload as I toiled long into each night. On press day the local head of BP, Peter Strickland, telephoned me repeatedly; each time I told my harassed secretary Beryl that I could not come to the phone, a new experience for him.

The souvenir issue, all 20 pages of it, wrapped round the usual newspaper, was a triumph. Exhausted from only two hours' sleep, I bore it proudly to the palace at Rifa'a. I was shown into the Ruler's private office and we sat together as he turned the pages. He stopped at an article on old Bahrain. 'But ... but ... this is my grandfather,' he said, as the photograph of Sheikh Hamed looked out at him. The black and white portrait of the old Ruler was by Vandyk, a society photographer of yesteryear London. The Ruler asked for a framed copy.

Again, the issue, so much the result of blood, sweat and tears, was a sell-out, even with extra copies printed. In shops all over the suq and across Bahrain, the front page was displayed prominently, in some cases even framed; thousands were airmailed to families and relatives all round the world. For me, it was the high water-mark of my editorship; to produce such an ambitious under-taking, in a tiny office and on a shoestring, spoke volumes for the growing power of our newspaper and our press. The front page hangs on the walls of my home to this day.

The other Arabic papers, by comparison, were eclipsed. The *Gulf Mirror*, I felt, had finally won its spurs. Congratulations poured in; Strickland, the local BP manager, apologised for his persistence on the paper's biggest day.

But as the accountants say, for every credit, there is a debit. Only a few days later I was summoned to the Ministry of In-formation for a courteous rebuke over an earlier edition: I had unwittingly given away the Hawar islands, the tiny archipelago off Bahrain's southern tip which had long been claimed by its neighbour Qatar – in illustrating an article, I had used a map from a Qatari publication showing the 16 Hawar islets as theirs.

I had been producing the *Gulf Mirror* more or less single-handed for many weeks, following the departure of my Indian assistant, Mr Thomas, who had finally felt that this sort of seat-of-your-pants newspaper work was not to his liking. I was becoming more and more worn out, and at last managed to persuade the board that the recruitment of another European was not just desirable but a necessity. I took an advertisement in the trade press magazine in Britain which drew an immediate response. The letters of application were a contrast in styles, from highly polished (very few) to ill-spelt and badly presented. One writer, who reminded me that we had met some years previously, had written on the back of a page torn out of a notebook, in pencil, and ended his brief note saying: 'Sorry about this scrawl but I'm in a hurry.' When I thought of the blood and tears I had shed over my own job applications in years past, I was almost ashamed at this lack of professionalism.

But there were some encouraging responses and these I winnowed down to a handful. I wanted a single person, having resolved not to employ anyone with a wife and family, firstly because of the cost of the air fares and secondly because I felt the whole newspaper project was still relatively high risk and wanted to limit the responsibility for luring someone away from a secure job in Britain to face the possible prospect of being left high and dry on a desert shore.

Interviews were set up and I managed to take three days off to fly to London. One by one, the job-seekers filed into my room in a hotel in Victoria, and one by one I had to rule them out at this face-to-face interview stage, for a variety of reasons. Some were clearly in trouble, fleeing broken marriages or debt collectors and seeking a refuge overseas; others displayed a close acquaintance-ship with drink, and yet others made clear they were doing me a favour even in turning up. One of the last people I saw was an Australian working in London as part of the usual walkabout by young people from Down Under who wanted to see the world before settling down at home. Ron Holdsworth, from *The Age* newspaper in Melbourne, had what it took; he spoke my language and wanted the chance to work in the Middle East as a mid-point on his return journey home. In his mid-twenties, he was married

GULF WEEKLY

MIRROR

**1961-1971
The Years
of
Progress**

Telephone : Manama 4324

Sunday, December 12, 1971. NO. 50   PRICE 100 FILS BD, 1 QDR, 65 FILS KD, 85 BAISAS RS

National Day supplement

Portrait of His Highness the Amir
taken specially for the Gulf Mirror

The souvenir issue produced to mark the tenth anniversary
of the Ruler's accession

but happy to meet the cost of his wife's fare. He accepted the job and it was agreed that he would start in a month's time.

Back in Bahrain, we arranged accommodation in a central flat and counted the days until his arrival. Ron, lean and stringy, with piercing blue eyes and a mass of black curly hair, proved a good choice and he met the challenge of this very unorthodox job with enthusiasm. His wife Ally, petite and attractive and herself a journalist, managed to find herself an office job and they settled down quickly. Production work went with a much more polished swing and Ron entered into island life with gusto, enjoying to the full the innumerable cocktail parties, finding a handy niche in his spare time at a favourite table in the bar lounge of the Gulf Hotel and frequently turning up in the morning hungover and unshaven, to which I was happy to turn a blind eye. We'd all been there.

As the weeks went by, Ron and Ally met and befriended a young Pakistani boy and quickly enthused him with tales of life in Australia. The lad, an unskilled worker, jumped at the chance to go there and Ron busied himself in his spare time with approaches to the Australian Trade Commission and securing a sheaf of official forms to make this dream come true. But it was all in vain; the lad had none of the basic qualifications required and the hard word was not long in coming. Tears all round, and a shattering blow for the boy who had allowed himself to believe that he was on his way to a promised land. For Ron, wild-eyed with rage at the way he thought his homeland had let him down, there was a daily tirade at the intransigence of his countrymen.

He was proving a strong support in the running of the news-paper but as the months went by, the lure of home became stronger and stronger and eventually he and Ally decided to continue their journey, this time back to Melbourne. As a farewell present I gave him a set of cufflinks of mother of pearl encased in 22-carat gold, as a memento of his time in Bahrain. Working with Ron was always like experiencing life on the edge of a hurricane, but I was sorry to see him go.

CHAPTER NINETEEN

Circulation was climbing, advertising revenue was healthy, the printing press and I had gradually evolved a working pattern that, though still arduous, did lead to improvements and, best of all, the newspaper was popular. But storm clouds were gathering. I had been asked to introduce a small Comment feature each week, giving the *Gulf Mirror*'s views on current events, and readily agreed. After all, this is part of what a local paper is all about. I can say that I did notice a certain reserve on the part of the Foreign Minister, the wily Sheikh Mohammed bin Mubarak, probably the leading diplomat in the Gulf, when I told him of this at our regular formal Thursday morning meetings in Government House.

At first the Comment pieces were innocuous, written by myself, of course. But then I was told by one of the paper's directors that this would not do. He wanted articles to be more forthright, attacking the government's stance on a range of subjects with, he stressed, no punches pulled. Now in taking the job as founding editor, I understood completely that our duty was to provide both news and a degree of entertainment. In terms of newspapers, Bahrain was a relatively young country; press freedom as we knew it in Britain lagged someway behind. The government in Bahrain was stern when any Arabic publication overstepped the mark. In the case of the *Gulf Mirror*, the editor was not a local but an expatriate. I was under no reservations about what would happen if I began to tweak the establishment's tail: a one-way ticket for me and my family out of the sheikhdom, with no likelihood of compensation from the paper's owners.

I had been told that the first of these new-style hard-hitting Comment pieces was expected to appear in the following week's issue; I was given the subject – some recent official ruling which I had been told to attack. This was journalism's equivalent of a rock and a hard place; if I refused, I would be sacked; if I complied, I would also inevitably be sacked. I pondered the problem. Then I remembered the Ruler's words at our first meeting: 'If you have any problems, come to me.' I drove to the palace and requested a private meeting. As I sat with Sheikh Isa, sipping the ritual coffee, I broached the subject, and my reluctance to comply, and the expected consequences. The smile abruptly left his face, to be replaced by a black frown. 'What do these people know of producing a newspaper?' he said contemptuously. 'You were right to come to me. Do not trouble yourself further. You will hear no more of this.' He was still angry when I took my leave.

He was right. I did not hear of it again. It was never mentioned. Life went on, the newspaper continued to appear weekly, and I discreetly dropped the short-lived Comment feature. No one noticed. That little episode marked the end of any direct interference over editorial content by directors. Trouble was to rumble on, I found, but underground. Months later, I heard through my sources that the board members concerned had been duly summoned and given what we in England like to refer to as a good kicking. The wise Prime Minister, Sheikh Khalifa, was also in my corner. 'You must make your nerves cold,' he counselled.

But what I thought had been a decisive battle turned out to be a curtain-raiser to more problems. In the frenetic business world of Bahrain, where profits were measured in staggeringly high double-digit percentages, certain of the newspaper's board had begun to complain loudly – loud enough for their grumblings to be picked up by other Arabic weeklies – about the slow progress towards making money. Yes, we were in overdraft, but whoever heard of a newspaper, without any subsidy from the government – that was to come in years ahead – moving into profit within years, never mind less than twelve months.

I was summoned and quizzed sharply about overheads, contributions and payments. In vain I protested that the staffing was shoestring, just myself and an assistant, the contributors – where they were paid at all – were paid woefully inadequately, and they were getting a professional product at a rock bottom price. It is worth mentioning that in years ahead, the *Gulf Mirror*, with a greatly expanded staff, began to turn in annual profits more than ten times the initial stake of each shareholder. Not a dinar of that was ever ploughed back.

The groundswell of grumblings continued, if anything even louder. I decided to take action. I drew up a confidential report for the board, setting out exactly why the paper was slowly struggling to get on its feet, how revenue was haemorrhaging because of the existing monopoly arrangements over advertising and how the potential for cash generation was failing to be exploited. Maintaining a low-key and pragmatic tone, I castigated every area of activity, from the printing press – 'inherently inefficient' – to lack of boardroom expertise in publishing an English-language newspaper, and to the outside advertising agency tasked with selling space with just one representative.

My report read:

A penetrating study into the finances and organisation of the *Gulf Mirror* now seems necessary, if the Gulf Publishing Company can hope to operate a modern and viable newspaper, in view of the rapidly mounting overdraft. A major weakness concerns the arrangement for handling advertising. As it stands, too large a slice of all advertising revenue is being diverted from the paper.

This arrangement has two important results affecting local and overseas advertising respectively. As far as local advertising is concerned, Media Representatives take a commission (previously 15 per cent, now 20 per cent) on all advertising going into the paper from whatever source. Thus, an advertisement placed through any other agency carries double commission.

As far as overseas advertising is concerned, Media Represent-atives have entered into an exclusive arrangement with a single advertising agency in Britain, whereby the latter handle all foreign advertising. Whatever terms were agreed in return for this exclusivity, they cannot be of benefit to the *Gulf Mirror*. (Countries such as Australia and a number of large international advertisers such as major airlines are handled locally through Media Representatives).

The general effect of these arrangements is to deprive the Gulf Publishing Company of a large reservoir of advertising revenue which would ordinarily be available from several agencies. These revenues would normally be regarded as the lifeblood of any English-language newspaper operating overseas.

The viability of the newspaper is adversely affected by four important factors:

A   Too little effort has been made by those responsible to promote sales of the newspaper through the Gulf, with the effect that the *Gulf Mirror* has made hardly any impact on this very important market, both in sales and advertising.

B   The cost of printing the paper is ludicrously high, mainly because of the inherent inefficiency of the existing printing facilities. Despite experience gained over the past year, the results in terms of improved efficiency and cost reduction are practically nil. Cheaper and better means of printing the paper should be considered as a matter of urgency.

C   At present board decisions are made without the benefit of expert knowledge of the complexities of running an English-language paper. Although the *Gulf Mirror* and the Gulf Publishing Company both have considerable potential for constructive development, it is difficult to see how this potential can be realised unless expert knowledge of English newspaper management is brought in at board level.

D   Unlike similar newspapers elsewhere in the world, the *Gulf Mirror* has no advertising staff of its own. All advertising services are in the hands of an outside company with only one representative; further, the paper cannot enjoy the sole attention of this representative and advertising has slumped significantly when he has been engaged on other projects unconnected with the Gulf Publishing Company. This dissipation of advertising effort represents another crucial element affecting profitability.

It is suggested that the entire existing advertising set-up be dismantled; all arrangements affecting the *Gulf Mirror* be cancelled; and the advertising side be absorbed completely by the Gulf Publishing Company itself. All future advertising arrangements should be worked out by a committee of the directors in consultation. Studies of alternative production facilities should also be made with a view to achieving more realistic printing charges.

Failing this, it is difficult to see how the board can hope to change the present situation.

It was all stating the obvious. My report was hand-delivered to each director, and a copy provided quietly to Bapco, which could always be relied upon to provide sage counsel from the sidelines. There was not a little anger from me in penning this incendiary document. I had succeeded in confronting and overcoming almost impossible odds to produce the *Gulf Mirror*, despite being seemingly handicapped and hamstrung at every turn. If the directors wanted to know why the money was not pouring in – though revenue was slowly increasing – I would tell them, I thought, in no uncertain terms.

The report's delivery marked the final rift between Belgrave and myself; relations were afterwards to be at arm's length. Granted, he had been instrumental in creating the foundations for the project, but the paper had arrived on the news stands without any prior publicity, aimed at readers who had not even known of its existence until the first issue. There had been no fliers, no announcements, and no promotion. To say a public relations agency had been involved, such inertia could hardly be credited. As Albert Healey, the shrewd Argentinian-born Scot jointly at the managerial helm of the Kanoo group, observed: 'Dear old James gives a whole new dimension to the meaning of the word procrastination.'

The board met, the report was discussed, I was questioned. What then happened? Nothing. A not untypical reaction among Bahrainis when faced with something requiring confrontation and distasteful decisions. After my next meeting with Sheikh Mohammed bin Mubarak, as I left his office, he turned to me, wire-rimmed spectacles glinting, and gave me a large wink. And the chorus of protest over profits? That too eventually went away. As for myself, who had had to contend with all these noises off and produce a newspaper, I went about my usual busy-ness with a slightly lighter step. Clearly, there was more to producing a newspaper in the Arab world than had been dreamt of in my philosophy, to borrow from *Hamlet*.

But if I thought I was away from dangerous rocks and now in safe water, as I piloted this cumbersome ship that was the *Gulf Mirror*, then I was dangerously mistaken. Little did I know, with days full of distraction that demanded my full attention, that an ambush lay ahead. Worn out by months of over-work and guerrilla warfare, the prospect of six weeks' leave, back to England and a change to recharge my batteries, gleamed like a beacon of hope, or more appropriately, an oasis in the distance, glimpsed through the hazed eyes of a desert traveller. It wasn't a mirage, but it could well have been. The people I had fallen out with on the board had been busy behind the scenes. What better way to control costs, they argued to fellow members, than to cut back on the terms and conditions of the editor himself? A new contract was drawn up, and with just days before we were due to go on leave, it was presented to me. The shock was considerable.

The terms on which I had been engaged had been changed.

Most important, my leave entitlement was altered. Instead of six weeks every 18 months, it became two months, but after two years of service. What does a difference of six months matter, the troublesome directors reasoned. But in the climate of Bahrain, the workload and the stress, it meant everything. It meant working another six months before I could go on leave. By contrast, staff with the island's major employers at that time were entitled to annual leave back in Europe every 12 months. Moreover, my terms and conditions of employment had been unilaterally changed and, at the very least, politeness dictated that I should have been consulted. It was a case of force majeure.

Having been to the Ruler once, I felt I had used my 'Get out of jail card'. Arab proverbs had helped me greatly during my time in Bahrain, and indeed ever since. The appropriate one in this case was 'Never use your sword too often, lest it become blunt'. So that ruled out Sheikh Isa. What was I to do? I was exhausted but not too tired to realise I had been outmanoeuvred. And I was neither ready to leave Bahrain, nor ready to admit defeat at the hands of a minority. They may have been few, but it seemed they had a disproportionate clout.

I changed our leave from six weeks to two months, proposing that two weeks of this be unpaid. The board agreed. I signed the document. It was a bad way to start a holiday. What lay ahead, I thought, would be dealt with in due course.

CHAPTER TWENTY

On my return, it was back to the old routine. Week relentlessly followed week but for every setback there always seemed to be a compensation; our own brief weekends, barely a day, had an idyllic quality and my escapes out of Bahrain and away from routine had been welcome breaks. Some of the most delightful times were the Eid festivals, with their three-day holidays, though it was business as usual for the newspaper. Ramadan, the month of fasting, where eating, drinking and smoking are suspended, by Moslem law, from the time when it is possible to distinguish between a white and a black thread as dawn breaks, could be trying for the Bahrainis. By day they seemed to be sleep-walking, waiting for the sunset when they could break their fast. The last meal of the night was just before sunrise, perhaps 4.45. The end of daylight would be announced by a British 25-pounder fieldgun, fired by the Defence Force; its thud, sending small boys scattering and once rocking my car when I ventured too close, could be heard in the middle of the island. But Ramadan was also a time of joy, with a warmth and closeness as families strolled on the streets after dusk, visiting friends, gossiping, and eating endlessly, and with good reason. Not everyone fasted, of course, but few dared to admit it.

As the new moon was sighted, marking the end of Ramadan and the start of Eid-al-Fitr, children would appear in their new clothes, sweets would be handed round and there would be an endless tour of formal visits by myself, on behalf of the news-paper, starting with the Ruler at Rifa'a and then continuing around all the prominent merchants and, of course, our friends. For the feasting, there were special dishes, a lamb stuffed with chickens, which were in turn stuffed with hard-boiled eggs, and with the rice inside the lamb containing spices, dates and raisins. It was always necessary to carry out two rounds of visits, for while Sunnis recognise the authority of Saudi Arabia on the appearance of the moon, for the Shias it must be visible in Bahrain.

By contrast, Muharram, the first month in the Islamic calendar, is a solemn time, with the Shias of Bahrain in mourning for their martyrs more than fourteen centuries before; the harrowing story of their deaths is retold long into the nights by mullahs in the mosques across the island, and how Ali and his family were set aside by others who became the early Caliphs. By the tenth of Muharram, with police standing uneasily by, the mourners, men, women and children, form a long winding procession with drums, chanting and wailing. Christine and our children were allowed to watch this, hidden on a rooftop in Manama, enveloped in black abbas, as the procession proceeded beneath them, with men flailing their backs with metal whips, cutting their foreheads with swords and striking their chests with their fists.

As years went by, fervour had increased and blood streamed from many of the marchers, dripping from their clothes and on to the street; it is no exaggeration to say that the gutters that day ran with blood. Such was the tension that there were ugly scenes when Europeans tried to take photographs, which was strictly illegal. Their cameras were snatched from them and the film ripped out; many were lucky to escape with just a fright; their insensitive behaviour outraged devout Shias. As far as the newspaper was concerned, it was all grist to the mill, filling column inches.

As the tempo wound down, I was surprised to receive a phone call from Government House. A minister wanted to see me. This was unusual. I was puzzled. I was shown into his office, with the waters of the Gulf twinkling through the floor-to-ceiling windows. He inquired after my health; I inquired after his. Then he produced a copy of the last issue of the *Gulf Mirror* and tossed it on to his desk. 'Sometimes newspapers have a strange way of using photographs,' he observed. I said guardedly that, yes, that was a view. 'Take this,' he gestured. 'My photograph has appeared just like a postage stamp.'

I had used his picture as what is known as a 'column-breaker', to split up a long line of type, and it had appeared measuring about an inch and a half square. 'Hmm, well . . . ' I began. At this point the string of coral worry beads he had been toying with broke. The red beads scattered everywhere, over his massive desk and bouncing across the marble floor. He frowned, bent down to try to retrieve some and banged his head on his desktop; his head rope fell off and his voile headcloth became disarranged. He straightened up. We looked at each other. Then we both burst out laughing. The matter was not mentioned again and I took my leave. But I never used his picture like that again.

I'd always liked cars, and like many people had harboured a far-off dream of, one day perhaps, owning a Rolls-Royce. Little did I realise how close I was to achieving this. One prominent Bahraini had several of these beautiful sleek monsters and Jawad Al-Arrayed, on one of his usual visits to my home, asked casually as he sipped a coffee whether I would like to own one. The owner, it transpired, had been experiencing problems with servicing this very out-of-the-ordinary fleet and had become increasingly exasperated, so exasperated that he had decided to get rid of them. But a garage forecourt sale was out of the question; they would be offered instead to selected people, quietly, at a price that even I could afford. I was torn. Who would turn down a Rolls-Royce? It would be a dream come true. But this marque had always been associated with Bahrain's ruling class, and for me it would mean raising my island profile to an unacceptably high level. I agonised. Christine was resolutely against it. Sadly, I turned down the offer. Sometimes I still think of it wistfully.

The flow of visitors never ceased. From the House of Dior in Paris there was Pierre Graticola, a hustling and bustling international salesman who spent six months away from home each year, taking the Dior brand around the world. He presented me with a bottle of Eau Sauvage aftershave, after I told him that this was a little, shall we say, effeminate for British men. 'Mais non,' he protested. 'The ladies will love it.'

A gypsy scrap dealer from the home counties called at my office, introducing with pride his sixteen-year-old girlfriend. This was a man who knew how to make a fortune; from the British naval base at Jufair he bought a fully equipped floating workshop for just £3,000. Using the phone in my office, he sold it to a dealer in Bandar Abbas for £40,000. And for an encore, he spotted a large manganese bronze propeller on the dockside. That cost him £1,000; he found a buyer within two days in India, for £10,000. His verdict: 'Not a bad little trip. I think we deserve some fun now.' The girlfriend, in a vestigious dress that left little to the imagination, giggled.

Decidedly less welcome were the international fraudsters who arrived overnight, presented forged drafts to two leading banks, and collected 20,000 dinars in cash – £18,000. That night they flew down to Dubai and did exactly the same thing again, before the telephone lines could get busy, and flew out the same day. Even Gazi Jarrar, the Jordanian head of CID in Manama, who regularly supplied me with snippets for the paper, expressed grudging respect. 'That's class,' he said.

The newspaper was in its second year of existence and I had been running it as a one-man band editorially for some months. Various candidates had been put forward to join me as my new number two but all had proved lacking. Then we finally struck lucky. A young Englishman already working in the Gulf was looking for a change. Inquiries proved encouraging and the job was offered. Enter Stefan Kemball, an Essex boy in his late twenties who had been working in the Middle East since graduating from Cambridge. He had spent some time with the United Nations Relief and Works Agency, helping Palestinians in Beirut, before moving to a media job in Kuwait. With him was his Lebanese-Armenian wife Vera, petite, honey-blonde, vivacious and captivating.

Stefan quickly settled into the routine of producing a newspaper and rapidly proved his mettle by accepting without a flinch the handicaps involved. We proved a good team. I could be volatile and exuberant, while he was measured and thoughtful. But sometimes the roles could be reversed. There was a mini-drama at the press one Saturday evening. All the proofs were ready for pasting-up in the final pages, we thought we were well ahead, and looked forward to the possibility of getting away relatively early, say 3am. But where was the bride? Fikhri, our usually dependable paste-up graphic artist, wasn't there. The hours ticked by as we sat in the press office, unable to do anything. I continually ranted about his absence – no one seemed to know where he was – as I paced the floor, not quite kicking the furniture but certainly close to it. Stefan sat there quietly, eyes downcast. The atmosphere was electric. I was releasing my mounting anxiety with fearful curses; but in Stefan it was all boiling away inside him, and a head of steam was building up.

Suddenly, at 8pm, an unconcerned Fikhri strolled into the printing works. He had been to the cinema with his wife, it transpired. 'Ah Fikhri,' I cried, 'good to see you. We've been missing you. Now let's get down to work.' But this was not enough for Stefan, tension at pressure-cooker point. He sprang to his feet. 'Fikhri, you bastard, where the hell have you been?' he howled. The next moment, the two of them were standing eyeball to eyeball, spittle flying, as accusations and outraged innocence clashed. Gradually the air cleared, helped to some extent by my murmuring conciliatory words.

An hour later, Stefan having departed back to the newspaper office, Fikhri sidled up to me. 'Mr Kemball, he is a very bad man,' he whispered. 'Oh, he's not a bad chap,' I said airily. 'He can get a little upset, but don't worry. I'll have a quiet word with him and we can forget the whole thing.' Suitably soothed, Fikhri returned to his desk. Stefan by now had calmed down and I, who had been responsible for the whole imbroglio indirectly, managed to suppress a grin. Poor Stefan.

But my new-found colleague, half-Polish, proved a find. His contribution greatly relieved the burden on my shoulders, and we established a close working relationship that included some badly-needed hilarious moments. As I mentioned in an earlier chapter, one of our most fruitful contacts was Ron Hemp, the personnel manager for an American offshore drilling company. Now Ron had a broad East Anglian accent and this, I have to confess, I was prone to mimic. 'Hello Stefan,' I would drawl over the phone in an exaggerated Lowestoft burr, 'Ron Hemp here.' After catching him out initially, it became a catch phrase, and was to rebound on us all.

It so happened that a telephone bill for Stefan was delivered by mistake to the office of . . . yes, that's right, Ron Hemp. He picked up the phone and called Stefan's home. 'Ron Hemp here . . . ' The caller could get no further. Stefan's wife Vera cut him short. 'Alright Andrew, I know it's you.' 'Er no, I really am Ron Hemp,' the caller protested. 'Don't be so silly, Andrew,' she persisted, 'I know perfectly well it's you.' Again poor Ron tried to continue, and again he got nowhere. Finally he rang Stefan at the office. 'I've just rung your home number and your wife appears to think I'm Andrew Trimbee.' Ron explained about the wayward telephone bill. Then the phone rang again. This time it was Vera. 'Stefan,' she said in an injured tone, 'Andrew is playing a practical joke on me. He's been ringing me and trying to pretend that he's Ron Hemp.' 'Well, Andrew's sitting right next to me,' Stefan told her, and somehow managed to untangle this very silly case of crossed wires.

The admirable Ron never did know about this, perhaps thankfully. In due course Stefan took over from me as editor and proved a more than capable incumbent, and I went my separate way. The

Kemballs went on to have two lovely daughters and I became godfather to one of them.

But there was an amusing postscript. Many years later, when both Stefan and I were living back in Britain and had lost touch for a while, I managed to find the number of his house in Chelmsford, Essex. He picked up the phone. 'Hello Stefan,' I said in my feigned East Anglian accent, 'Ron Hemp here.' There was a silence. 'Andrew, it's you, you bastard,' he said. 'And I know it isn't Ron Hemp as I can see him mowing the lawn at his house two doors away.' By a rare coincidence, the Hemps and the Kemballs had ended up living not only in the same county, and not only in the same town, but in the same road.

CHAPTER TWENTY-ONE

I was again feeling the need for a break, and a break was what we had. Christine, with her usual classic timing, noted the signs of chronic fatigue, went to a friendly travel agent and bore back tickets in triumph. 'We're off to Shiraz,' she announced. 'A four-day break will work wonders for us all.'

Shiraz, fabled Persian city of nightingales, poetry, wine and a treasure trove of exquisite blue-domed mosques, lay across the Gulf, over a range of mountains, barely an hour's flight away by the twin-turbo-engined Fokker Friendships of Gulf Air.

No one had warned us about the turbulence. For 20 minutes, I experienced the worst buffeting, plunging and shuddering I had ever encountered; in the middle of all this, a visit to the tiny toilet was compelling. Someone later asked me to describe it: like trying to take a leak in a chamber pot while on the back of a bucking bronco, was how I summed it up.

In Shiraz, we had reservations at the central Park hotel, 'The only place to stay,' we had been advised. 'On no account stay at the Park Saadi.' The Park was full and had no record of our reservations, obviously a breakdown in communications. Fortunately the Park Saadi did have rooms and welcomed us with open arms; we soon realised we had had a stroke of luck. The hotel was a huge old period house in sprawling gardens flecked with snow; oranges still hanging on the trees lent a splash of colour to the late winter landscape. Our rooms were spacious, the corridors wide, and at the end, on each landing, sat a sinister little old woman, on our floor knitting as she mounted guard, in resemblance not unsimilar to Rosa Klebb, the Russian spy out of a James Bond film.

Then followed an idyllic four days; we toured the labyrinthine underground bazaar, lunching off mutton kebabs in a vaulted caravanserai filled with fierce-looking men in cloaks and those pie-crust hats always seen in television coverage of Afghanistan. The first day took us to the tented city where only months before the Shah had staged an extravaganza for the world's crowned heads in celebration of 2,500 years of imperial rule in Iran; the Duke of Edinburgh and Princess Anne had represented Britain's House of Windsor; the Queen stayed away, her presence considered a security risk by MI6. There was a replica of the Shah's peacock throne in the principal tent; I tried it for size, with a enterprising Polaroid photographer lurking nearby to sell us the instant pictures. Barely eight years later Mohammed Reza Shah Pahlavi, like another of his guests, Hailie Selassie of Ethiopia, would be gone. Another day, we toured the ruined city of Persepolis, a few miles outside Shiraz, with its magnificent carvings, pillars and statuary built by Darius the Great in the fifth century BC. I was able to keep my promise to a member of New York's Press Club when I was there. He asked that, if I ever visited Persepolis, to be sure to take a photograph of the name scratched on marble by Stanley, the great American journalist famous for ever for his words in darkest Africa: 'Dr Livingstone, I presume.' Pictures of the graffiti by this nineteenth-century vandal were duly posted back.

In the evening, looking for a diversion, we inquired about night life. 'No need to go anywhere,' we were told. 'The hotel has its own disco downstairs.' After our supper, washed down by the dark red wine of Shiraz, we headed for the disco, knowing our daughters were safely in their own room with Rosa Klebb on sentry duty. The music was deafening, the strobe lights blinding, and space to dance almost impossible to find as twisting, writhing bodies shook and lurched to the world's latest pop tunes. What made it unforgettable was the overpowering knock-a-buzzard-off-a-shitcart BO from both sexes that polluted every corner. We were glad to escape.

Across the road from the hotel was a high-walled garden with a tiny latch gate. Inside was another world, a lovely Persian garden, secluded, deserted and peaceful, a setting straight out of Omar Khayam, where I would sometimes escape to for an hour of tranquil solitude. Our little daughters found their own diversions; when not playing in the snow, making giant snowballs, they would stare fascinated at the two dwarves on duty in the hotel foyer. As they passed, each of my girls would cuff them smartly on the head; it was a novelty to find an adult smaller than them. Remonstrations by their shamed parents were ignored; the dwarves pretended they enjoyed it.

Shiraz was truly a magical city, though every fourth vehicle seemed to be a military truck, and every fourth person wore an army uniform. Our visit was all too short; it was time to return to dusty Bahrain. Home beckoned. I arrived back at the office for frantic days of catching up for the next edition, and was very rapidly briefed by the island's gossip mongers as to what had happened in my absence; Jean Thuillier had struck again, it seemed, trying the patience even further of his long-suffering airline boss, Alan Bodger. This time his irrepressible catering chief had surpassed himself. The airline's chairman, a pompous, overweight little man, had arrived from London on a visit; the usual five-star dinner had been laid on at the airport restaurant as he stepped off the VC10, with Thuillier stage-managing the whole evening.

Alas, Jean had over-imbibed as he and his staff waited for the jet to land; all caution was suppressed. As the VIP later got into a limousine with Bodger at the wheel, for the drive to his hotel, Thuillier thrust his perspiring head through the driver's window. 'Excuse me, Captain Bodger,' he bellowed, 'but tell the chairman he isn't likely find any women at this time of night.' The visitor was apopleptic, Bodger speechless. 'I just wanted the earth to open up beneath me,' he told me later. 'I had to give Jean a very public official carpeting the next day, in front of witnesses.' Such excruciating moments were the price he had to pay for his catering manager's wayward brilliance.

My diary reminded me of stories still to be written. First, our women's feature, and I had come up with what I thought was a more-than-usually interesting subject. One of the expatriate girls working in Bahrain was a willowy, striking-looking redhead. Knowing of our constant quest for stories, she told me that back in Britain, she had been a coal merchant, delivering house to house from a lorry. That whetted my appetite and we met at her home. The story, initially promising, turned out to be a complete dud; I just couldn't prise anything from her beyond the deadpan fact that this was a girl who had run a somewhat unusual business – for a girl. As I got up, putting away my notebook, I was wondering just how I could turn this into a read-me article and concluded that I probably couldn't. As I opened the door, she turned and said: 'There's something else that might interest you. I'm a clairvoyant.' How many times has that happened, when an unpromising chat suddenly turns up a nugget of gold? That was the story. It was a gift she had had all her life: give her a sealed envelope with a message inside, and she could tell you what it said; her cousin was married to Douglas Harding, an attache at the British embassy, as it now was; she warned her cousin, that he was to receive a phone call that morning that would bring difficulties – he came home for lunch in a very bad mood. 'Witch,' he commented. If witch she was, then she was a white witch, one of the nicest subjects of a *Gulf Mirror* article we ever had.

Douglas was not above being pompous, and made the mistake of turning up at a poolside party one afternoon wearing a lounge suit. For some reason we had words and Her Majesty's Commercial Representative ended up being thrown in the pool, fully clothed. He thereafter maintained a diplomatic silence over this incident.

The clairvoyant shared column space with two ground-breaking Bahraini women: Sourya Al-Safer, the island's first woman vet, petite, brunette, who grew up as a child with the small animals her father kept on his weekend farm; and Safia Dowaigher, young head of the women's teacher-training college, in Manama, who, along with Sourya, represented the new image of women in the Gulf, Mercedes-driving and a great follower of western fashion.

The previous teacher-training college in Manama had a chocolate-box appearance, with twin flights of steps running up the front and ornamental towers. It was the residence of a long-ago ruler who had asked his British adviser to design a new palace. The British scratched their heads; this was new territory for the civil engineers. Plans were sent for, from Delhi. The palace was completed, a replica of a Victorian railway station in the British Raj. His Highness seemed satisfied.

Other Bahrainis were also innovators, like the first local psychiatrist, in a field not readily understood, though with the island's changing face and modern heavy industry replacing largely traditional occupations, there had been an upsurge in mental health problems. 'My practice is growing,' he told me. 'But patients still leave their cars round the corner from my consulting rooms, just in case anyone sees them.'

Our happy return that week was marred by the sudden death of an old friend, a bon viveur whose heart had suddenly given out after years of high living. The funeral service at St Christopher's was sombre, the church packed with his friends from all round the Gulf, Arabs as well as fellow Britons. As companions of the dead man, an engineer, we had helped with arrangements with the vicar, a dour Ulsterman, lanky and stooping, known affectionately to his flock as Doctor Death.

Two days later, he rang Christine. 'I've got a date for the interment,' he told her in his broad Belfast brogue. 'It's all set up for tomorrow morning, so please be there in good time with the ashes.' 'Ashes?' she asked. 'What ashes? I haven't got them.' 'Oh dear,' he said, 'I don't seem to have them either.' 'What are we going to do?' she said. 'I'll just have to think of something,' he told her.

The next morning we were among a solemn party gathered around the sandy freshly-dug grave in the wind-blown Christian cemetery, isolated on open land some miles out of Manama. As the miniature casket was placed in the hole, his grief-stricken widow, tears pouring down her face, threw herself on it, calling out her husband's name. Doctor Death turned and looked at Christine, then rolled his eyes heavenward.

CHAPTER TWENTY-TWO

By now I had been in Bahrain for two years and I was becoming increasingly dissatisfied with my remuneration, poor by almost any standards for a European. I made discreet inquiries about the possibility of a rise; it was made clear that no rise would be forthcoming. I talked it over with Christine, and we agreed that this was not acceptable. It had been a roller-coaster ride in a desert island setting sometimes magical and always beautiful, with the Bahrainis themselves kind, compassionate and considerate, our very own version of 'One Thousand And One Nights'. But it was time to move on.

There had already been approaches: Bapco, knowing of my discontent, had sounded me out over a job in their public relations department; and the stalwart Abdulla Kanoo had phoned me from his office in Dammam, Saudi Arabia, saying that the Aramco oil company would give me a job at any time, such was the power of his reach. Later, in gratitude, though I never took the offer further, I gave him a pair of gold cufflinks. He had been a staunch ally.

Closer to home, the Alba aluminium smelter, just entering production and employing more than 2,000 people, mostly Bahrainis, was suffering from a woeful public reputation, with a high accident rate, arduous working conditions and a process that no one outside the industry understood. The smelter had been built by an international consortium, British, German and American, in partnership with the government, using the abundant natural gas to fuel the giant turbines that in turn generated the vast amount of electricity needed to reduce the fine alumina powder, imported from Australia, and persuade it to yield up aluminium, one of the world's wonder metals which commands a premium price. This was then cast into ingots and shipped out from the smelter's own artificial island.

The smelter's management agreed there was a serious problem over its image; I persuaded them to recruit me to do something about it, using my government contacts and my press links in Europe. The salary was agreed: more than double what the paper was paying me. But there was one hurdle to surmount. Among the smelter's directors was a senior government minister, a close friend of one of my old adversaries on the *Gulf Mirror*'s board. I had to outwit both of them and head off this particular problem well before it got to the pass.

Sayyed Mahmoud Al-Alawi, the Minister of Finance, a small, energetic Shia and probably the most respected man in the government, had become a close friend to both me and my family. He had served the Al-Khalifa since he was a boy and had a mind like a calculator. Years later, he was to be honoured by the Ruler with a gift of his own personal palace, as a reward for literally a lifetime of trusted service. We sat together at a private dinner given by Ahmed Kanoo. I told him of my dilemma. He listened carefully. 'You have nothing to worry about' was his only comment.

I heard later that at a board meeting of the smelter, in Lisbon, he had called senior staff over to him, in front of his fellow directors, and told them loudly: 'I am delighted that Mr Trimbee is joining us.' The matter was clinched; no one messed with Sayyed Mahmoud. In bridge terms, it was a grand slam. The job went through, and the contract was signed.

In the weeks before I left, returning for a much needed break to a Britain on the verge of joining the Common Market and going decimal – my family had gone back ahead of me – I thought it would be a nice nostalgic touch to stay with Ralph Izzard again. Neither of us got quite what we bargained for in an episode I shall term the curious incident of the rat in the night-time. Ralph, as ever somewhat straitened financially, had dispensed with his faithful Muscati and standards had suffered accordingly without Abdulla on sentry duty.

Each night saw a farewell party somewhere in Manama for me and, sleeping in one of the downstairs bedrooms, I woke around 3am with a raging thirst. The first night, in my bare feet, I walked into the kitchen to find something cool. As the fridge door creaked open, I became aware of something watching me. On the opposite wall, perched behind the wall heater, I saw the head and whiskers of what was clearly an oversize rat. The next morning I casually mentioned this to Ralph. 'Oh no, you're mistaken, old boy,' he said. 'Must have been a cat.'

The following night, the same scenario repeated itself. Thirst. Kitchen. Drink. Rat. And the morning chat with Ralph. After three days of this, Ralph was becoming irritated. I had clearly exceeded the boundary of what was considered house manners for a guest. But the night-time incidents continued, with Ralph getting crosser and crosser. The matter was abruptly resolved in my favour. One sunny wintry morning we were sitting chatting in his majlis area with both sets of doors open to the courtyard when, suddenly, a gigantic tree rat entered through one doorway, trotted nonchalantly past us, and exited stage right. There was a silence. 'I think I see what you mean,' Ralph conceded.

There was one poignant parting touch. Days before I was due to fly home, I received a summons to go to the palace at Rifa'a. The Ruler wished to see me. Once again I was shown into his inner office. He asked about my new job. 'You have had your share of troubles with the newspaper,' he told me, 'yet you overcame them. You have made many friends here. We are in your debt. We are pleased that you are coming back.' It was a touching moment with this dignified, caring man who, true to his word, had provided, quietly, essential support that had ensured the paper's survival. He reached down and handed me a little red box; inside was a solid gold Rolex watch. 'You are a Bahraini now,' he told me. 'You will never leave Bahrain.'

But before my job with Alba had even begun, we hit a snag. The smelter was paying the air tickets for me and my family from England, but that still left the trip back home, and the *Gulf Mirror's* directors, under the terms of my new contract, had no intention of helping out. Once again, Middle East Airlines came to the rescue, through their Bahrain manager, Fouad Habiby, who had become a friend. I explained the predicament as we sipped coffee in his office in the main Kanoo building. He was kindness itself. 'If Alba are paying for outward travel, back here,' he said, 'just get them to book the tickets through me and I'll take care of the rest.' He was as good as his word. What an airline, and what staff. No wonder I always insisted on travelling with them for the remainder of my time in the Gulf, paying full fare of course. Flying from the Gulf to London via Beirut, then known as the Paris of the Middle East, was an inconvenience; it meant a dog-leg over Saudi Arabia instead of taking a direct route, and added two and a half hours to the trip, taking into account transit time. But the MEA welcome, the service, and that tantalising glimpse from the air-port of beautiful Lebanon made it worth it.

The return flight from England turned out to be memorable. Cross-winds buffeted the MEA 707 as it made its approach to Beirut, flying in over an angry sea through flurries of snow. The Boeing rocked alarmingly as we approached the runway, almost on the edge of a cliff, as the Australian pilot fought to hold it steady. Suddenly he cut the power and we hit the ground with an almighty crash, landing so heavily that I was thrown bodily across the seats, ending up with my head on Christine's lap. From the galley came the sound of breaking crockery, and the overhead lockers burst open, showering passengers with raincoats, bags and even duty-free bottles. But all I could think of was, no matter what happens now, at least we're down. The jet crabbed violently from side to side as the brakes fought the fierce winds. Finally, it taxied in to the terminal. We descended the steps, holding on to each other as the gale raged, clutching at us. After that experience, certainly the worst landing I have ever experienced, I think I could be forgiven for fearing the worst when we took the connecting flight down to Bahrain. By contrast, the landing could not have been smoother, the wheels skimming the tarmac to touch down with scarcely any sensation. I have considered myself a connoisseur of landings ever since.

I was now about to enter the wild and woolly world of heavy industry, after years spent in the maelstrom of newspapers. But I took to it like a duck to water; I found I had a natural aptitude for this new environment. I came from an engineering family; my father, formerly with Rolls-Royce, had built up his own small machine-tool business in the West Riding of Yorkshire, and my brother was also a machine-tool engineer, joining in due course the board of a British company selling high-end Japanese multi-lathes, computer-controlled, where you didn't get much for less than a million dollars. Cutting oil, I used to say, was in my blood.

For the first few weeks, until our company villa was ready for occupation, we were put up in some style at the still new Gulf Hotel. That first morning, as I drove the 12-mile route to the smelter, joining a stream of other cars, ready to start work at 7am, all I could think of was: am I really going to do this journey for the next five years (the qualifying period for the company's very generous provident fund)? The answer was yes. I was shown to my office, relatively small, in a row roughly built from breeze blocks, with steel windows and a corrugated roof. As an introduction to the company and all its works, I was handed an intimidating pile of internal memos and correspondence. For the next few hours I waded through this mass of paperwork, painstakingly at first, then rapidly, and then skipping. By the end of that first day I was pretty much in the picture.

And it was a rather depressing one. It was clear that despite the vital local gas, despite the massive amount of electricity generated, and the mountain of alumina imported annually, this was a project that ran on paper. Never before or since have I experienced such a daily outpouring of memos, correspondence, directives, inter-departmental briefings, and pompously and meticulously annotated missives from personnel, a veritable daily blizzard blowing from the mail room and forming drifts on my desk, no doubt equivalent to the annual felling of a small forest. For someone used to employing a professional paucity of words, never using three when one would suffice, it was awesome, and in time I was to discover that this obsession with paperwork was in fact a smokescreen for a lack of real work by middle management, part of a culture of quite grotesque over-staffing. I rapidly evolved a way of dealing with this daily waste of time: I would let the paperwork pile up in my in-tray until it reached an impressive height, then start another pile. If, after three or four weeks, I heard nothing more about the subjects raised, then I would lift up the earlier pile and dump it with a crash into the waste basket. It was a solution that never failed.

The smelter, with a capacity at full production of 120,000 tons – this was later to more than double – was supplied with its raw material, alumina, from Australia. This fine white powder was delivered by bulk carrier to the smelter's own manmade island. In this massive equation of supply and demand, it was always cheaper to bring the alumina to the power, even if it meant shipping it halfway across the world.

Because of a reluctance by competitors to sell Alba the best technology, the process was at the bow and arrow stage and the smelter had a serious safety problem in those early days. Accidents were commonplace, with occasional fatalities. That was one of the reasons for my appointment. Not only had I to improve the image of the plant locally and internationally, but I had to help raise the awareness of our Bahraini workforce, whose attitude to danger in those pioneering days could be indifferent or even downright foolhardy. The days were long, working from 7am until 4pm, but I rarely got away until much later. My own fault. In later years I would have realised that quality counts for more than quantity, but there was no denying that the nature of my job meant I could not expect to work only the set hours; much of my work was outside the plant, in the world that lay beyond.

In the evenings, life continued as normal: cocktail parties, dinners, socialising, which took no account of the fact that no matter how late the evening became, the alarm clock went off at 5.40am, just time for a shave, coffee and light breakfast before jumping into my car at 6.20am to drive to work. For non-shift workers, Alba worked a five-day week, with Thursdays and Fridays free. But every Thursday morning was spent on my 'calls', making the long round of friends, contacts and officials in Manama and the suq, exchanging gossip, picking up news, touching base, for these people contributed to my essential stock-in-trade: inside information.

As operations at the smelter began to stabilise, after the usual crop of start-up problems, when things either did not work as they were supposed to, or the staff didn't, curious visitors and VIPs started to arrive, first a trickle then a steady stream. They were a nuisance but a necessary one; Alba was a showcase for the first major piece of diversification in the Gulf and people wanted to know all about it, and whether it really was a white elephant, as the sceptics had been saying. One of the prime movers behind Alba was Paul Brauner, an entrepreneur and metal trader based in London and Switzerland; testimony to the fact that Alba was no white elephant could be found in his next project, the even bigger smelter in Dubai; both became among the most productive – and profitable – in the world.

The British embassy was constantly on the phone to me, wanting to show visiting businessmen just what was being achieved. When visitors stopped off in Bahrain and paid their usual courtesy call to Her Majesty's representative, embassy staff simply did not know what to do with them beyond the ritual coffee and possibly dinner. Alba was heaven sent. Instead of wasting their time, these visitors could waste ours. Many of them, bankers, traders, sometimes captains of industry, or just carpet baggers, had made Bahrain their last stop after a prospecting trip down the Gulf. They usually gave themselves just one day, Friday, returning home that night to enjoy their own weekend before work as usual on Monday. Friday of course was our equivalent of their Sunday; a day of rest. Supposedly. Time and again I was dragged away from home and family at short notice. Finally, I had words with the charge d'affaires. 'It's hardly asking much,' he spluttered. 'What's a couple of hours?' 'Put it this way,' I told him. 'What do you think would happen if I rang the head of a major British company on a Sunday and told him I wanted to see round his operation – now. Even the mildest of men would have little difficulty in telling me to fuck right off.'

And that's what I did in future, these well-intended and thought-less visits having drained dry my well of goodwill. I firmly turned down the next few requests for a Friday visit. And after a while the embassy stopped asking. 'Can't think why you didn't tell 'em earlier,' Otto Von Drack, our American production head, on secondment from Kaiser, told me. 'To produce aluminium you need to develop a thick skin.'

It's true the American way of doing things differed greatly from the British, and trying to reconcile the two views was not always easy. Even our blunt Yorkshire foremen found they could learn a thing or two from Yank counterparts. 'You've got to learn to cuss and swear,' a Kentucky-born potroom charge-hand told me. 'If you want to make a point, first of all you have to get people's attention.'

Our American colleagues were a colourful crew. They could be trying, and I know they said the same about the assorted Brits and Europeans they had to work with. To a man, I always found them helpful, and off the plant they displayed that typical American bigness of heart that makes them so endearing. There was Pat Davey, whisps of ginger hair covering his balding pate, fresh from the Kaiser smelter in Ghana. He was Alba's first operations manager under a technology agreement with Kaiser. Pat was a little flamboyant when he changed out of his working clothes; for formal occasions, he was extremely proud of his glaring blue suit, made up for him by an African tailor. To Brits of a certain age, remembering the immediate post-war Tate & Lyle 1lb packets of sugar, it was always known as his 'sugar bag suit'. He used to say: 'Compared with Ghana, Bahrain's a picnic. They had no money to spend on lunatic asylums. I used to see mentally disturbed Africans wandering down the road, stark naked, dongs flapping.'

When his tour of duty ended, he was succeeded by Bill Armantrout, who commuted every fortnight from a smelter in West Virginia. Armantrout had a different style to Pat's; he was cool, laid back, thoughtful and stroked smooth the ruffled feelings that Pat had left in his wake. He lived this exhausting migrant life for nearly a year, then handed over to Otto Von Drack who flew in, looked around, and decided he liked what he saw and wanted to stay. Otto again was completely different; he had headed the Kaiser smelter in Tacoma, Washington, and had left behind his beloved yacht. He swapped it for his golf clubs and would play on the 18-hole Awali sand course each Friday with his wife – he termed it 'the torture course'. Otto was the epitome of an American gentleman. His Czech immigrant father had had a furniture business in New York. 'He'd worked for himself for so long that when his business collapsed, he was unemployable,' Otto would reminisce. 'Being your own boss is great – as long as the money comes in. If it stops, then it isn't a lot of fun.'

His progress up through Kaiser had been rapid. Kaiser needed someone who could work alongside Europeans without fearing a new world war. Otto had cut his teeth on the Anglesey smelter in Wales. He was a natural choice for Bahrain: horses for courses, and in the furnace heat of a Bahrain summer he rarely broke a sweat. 'Everyone knows what they're supposed to be doing. By and large, I just let them get on with it.' That was his formula, and it turned out to be a winning one. Otto was that rare thing, a natural leader of men. And he had learned the hard way. As a wartime pilot for the United States, he had flown the lumbering DC-3 workhorses over the Hump air route into China, carrying supplies and ammunition as part of a shuttle delivery service in the war against the Japanese.

Nearly thirty years later, he found he had an afternoon to spare, he told me. He was driving past an airfield in the States. On a whim, not having flown since 1945, he drove through the gates, had a medical check, and an hour later was airborne at the controls of a little trainer, admittedly with an instructor at his side. 'It all came flooding back,' he recalled. 'Flying's just like riding a horse, you never forget it. If you do something wrong, you can come down to earth with a bump. But I managed a perfect landing. That satisfied my curiosity. I've never piloted an aircraft since.'

These were people at the sharp end. But at Alba's board level, people who visited Bahrain regularly were of a different calibre. There was a grizzled financier who never spoke to anyone, much to the irritation of fellow Americans who shared accommodation with him at the Alba guesthouse. He regularly took umbrage at expenditure on anything but production matters, begrudging any-thing spent on entertainment. At one of the lavish dinners to mark the end of a board meeting, one of his director colleagues mischievously drew his attention to the price of a bottle of French wine standing on the table. I should mention that at this time, the world price of aluminium had gone into freefall. He snatched up the bottle, pushed his spectacles up on the top of his head, and thrust his face at the label, squinting his eyes. 'Forty dollars?' he exclaimed. 'It cain't be true.' It wasn't. Watching him, Christine had played a little practical joke; she had surreptitiously taken the bottle and written the price on it with a ballpoint. There was a culture of corporate extravagance even during these relatively hard times which he tried and failed to curtail. Eventually he got tired of trying and sold his shareholding.

These were international big-hitters, travelling from continent to continent to oversee their investments, and the men charged with looking after them. But Jaime Ortes Patino was in a class of his own. Patino, short, somewhat rotund and modestly dressed, was a descendant of the legendary Bolivian 'Tin King' Patino and by any standards something of a latter-day oligarch; his family still held sway in Latin-America but this Patino was of a new generation, based in Paris and flying each week by Concorde down to Rio. Keeping a tight rein on his family interests was a seven-day-a-week job. He was almost permanently in the air, When he arrived in Bahrain, I was there to meet him and we established a rapport immediately. I handed over a selection of books about the island and its history to this little figure in a raincoat and open-necked shirt: his habitual travel attire, at a time when business people around him always wore a tie. We drove up to the plant and he embarked on a round of meeting management, looking at the books and a very cursory plant tour.

Everyone was in awe of this man with a legendary family whose financial clout was more than all the other directors combined. The finale of his visit was the ritual lavish dinner at the Gulf Hotel, men only, attended by senior staff. The day's work over, Patino settled down to enjoying himself and that meant, it quickly became apparent, having several drinks. This mild-mannered man changed in front of our eyes to a very definitely opinionated and truculent guest who was not used to anyone having a contrary view.

As he mounted one of his hobby horses, the world's press, he held forth uninterrupted, naturally. No one was going to contradict him. Except me. 'Would you agree with me, Andrew?' he directed at me. 'No I certainly don't,' I replied forthrightedly. 'Well, I never expected you to, anyway.' And then I took over. In my role at the smelter, if I didn't have a licence to kill, then I did have a licence to do virtually whatever I liked, within reason, as a government-approved appointee. The room fell silent. I waxed on about the need for a vigilant press, even if it managed to upset people in carrying out its role as a watchdog. Patino spent most of his time talking to me after that exchange. We ended the evening with both of us worse for wear.

Next morning I drove him to the airport. It was exit the Demon King. He never paid a second visit, and whatever he had seen cannot have impressed him. He sold his family's shareholding soon after; it was taken up by the government. His loss, their gain. The smelter was to turn if not into a gold mine, then certainly an immensely profitable enterprise. Those who kept faith reaped the reward; the fainter hearts who fell by the wayside saw a scant return.

CHAPTER TWENTY-THREE

As a workforce, the Bahrainis proved adaptable, gradually moving into management roles until, some twenty years later, the first Bahraini was appointed Alba's general manager. Abdul-Karim Salimi had carved out his own path with a single-minded determination, moving to France, where he married a local girl, and returning years later to his home country to become initially head of maintenance at Alba. The smelter was a ready employer of both sexes. Girls, bright and eager to learn, and also eager to earn money, found jobs in the offices, and they were ambitious. Soon we had girl trainee engineers and trainee nurses. Many went on to qualify.

Salimi was a highly-disciplined self-starter. When Ahmed Al-Absy, a friend of mine, was appointed the new head of public relations, Salimi welcomed the former defence force officer and told him: 'I'm sure we can work well together. I've never been late for work in my life.' He was no match for the sharp-as-paint Ahmed, who told him: 'We'll be a good combination. I've never been on time in my life.'

As we moved up to full production, the flow of visitors increased both in frequency and in rank. Kurt Waldheim, the former head of the United Nations, arrived, his tall stooping figure very recognisable from the television news. He appeared impressed. Only later did his background return to haunt him when it was disclosed that the head of the world's biggest humanitarian body, and later president of Austria, was suspected of involvement in Nazi humanitarian crimes, as an officer in the German Wehrmacht, and he was barred from the United States. Robert Menzies, the former Australian prime minister, arrived one week, slow-talking and humorous. A major statesman, and no skeletons in his cupboard. At least, none we ever heard of.

From the sublime to the ridiculous to the downright unpleasant. One day we were contacted by the government's head of protocol who told us to prepare for an extremely important visitor. The wail of the police sirens could be heard miles away as the motorcade approached, lights flashing and dust billowing. The leading limousine drew up outside our offices. An African retainer sprang from the front seat and deferentially wrenched open the passenger door. Out stepped a tiny man, immaculately dressed. It was President Omar Bongo of Gabon, circled by a crowd of bodyguards and retainers. He exuded an air of menace. After visiting management, we prepared for the plant tour. This little man, cocky and arrogant, wore built-up shoes, I noticed. As we made the various stops around the plant, he became more and more difficult. His murderous-looking minders were menacing, and themselves frightened of their master, whose whims could change at a moment. Halfway through the tour, I had had enough. I started to treat him with an off-hand insolence. He noticed straight away, and so did his guards. I don't think he had ever been treated to such a display of polite scorn in his life. He bristled, his thugs squirmed, and there was nothing they could do about it. For him it had indeed been a visit to remember, for perhaps the wrong reasons. And for myself, I made a firm mental note never to visit Gabon. If this head of a small West African country had come to Bahrain in the hope of a handout, he had miscalculated. Bahrain may have been the first country in the Gulf where oil was discovered, but it had no money to spare for a sizeable donation to an importuning country.

Princes, rulers, sheikhs, we saw them all, personalities big and small. After visiting the ruler and senior ministers, they were directed to Alba as a useful way of filling in the greater part of a day for guests who were largely unbidden and unwanted but always, in the great Arab tradition, made welcome.

One of the most memorable was Muhamed Ali, the former Cassius Clay, world heavyweight boxing champion and a convert to Islam, who was touring the Middle East with a large retinue. The 'Louisville Lip' lived up to his nickname. Surrounded by local journalists, he treated them to a non-stop display of repartee which had them equally amused and baffled. One reporter thrust his way to the front of the crowd of pressmen. 'Ali, I used to box,' he faltered. Ali turned his amused gaze on him. 'Oh yeah?' he asked. 'What did you box, apples and oranges?' There was an appreciative roar from the crowd. The reporter turned to me: 'What did he mean? How can you box oranges?' There's no answer to that, as comedians of the time would say.

The big names came, and went. When the British Airways Concorde made its official inaugural flight to Bahrain, on board was a collection of worthies, household names and personalities, who were lined up to meet local dignitaries at a large reception. A tiny woman with a petite hour-glass figure, wearing a black couture cocktail dress, took my hand. 'I'm Margaret, Duchess of Argyll. And you?' Margaret, who had achieved an impressive degree of notoriety in Britain's News of the World for her sexual exploits and dalliances, was impressive and intimidating. Her little black eyes bored into me with the gaze of a predator, assessing me, so I thought. In the best tradition of News of the World reporters, I made my excuses and left, after passing her on to another unsuspecting guest.

The Concorde visit was all grist to the mill for Alba, as far as I was concerned. With the help of the island's Post Master, Ricky Thorpe, I brought out a stamp collector's first-day cover to mark the occasion, linking the smelter with the world's most famous aircraft, built of aluminium of course. We produced hundreds of these envelopes, bearing a commemorative special stamp. They were sent around the globe from Bahrain, every single one was snapped up, and for months afterwards we received requests from philatelists worldwide for the special envelope, definitely a one-off and a feather in the cap for this strange company in a faraway land.

We also exerted a strange fascination for the Far East, and became a regular stopping-off point for deputations from Japanese companies. For these visits they invariably arrived mob-handed, anything up to ten or more, all with notebooks and tape-recorders, making copious observations. Language could be a problem; not all spoke English. After one comprehensive and lengthy walk around the smelter, a spokesman stepped forward. 'Very impressed,' he told me. 'But have one question.' I waited. The spokesman fumbled for words. 'What about punishment?' I was taken aback. Visions of ritual beheadings flashed through my mind. Then I twigged. He was asking about disciplinary procedures. Like the film starring Bill Murray, years later, some things are simply lost in translation.

Coming to grips with a different culture and indeed different customs could bring problems. One Japanese visitor, a represent-ative of a metal-buying customer in Tokyo, was taken on a night out by the head of our shipping department. Both drank not wisely but a little too well. Our man was well used to this sort of endurance course; not so the visitor. At the end of the evening, as they stood outside a restaurant, he told his host: 'Excuse me, I want to retire.' 'So do I,' agreed Alba's man of the moment, 'but unfortunately I'm not old enough.' At that moment, his guest turned away and was violently ill across the pavement. 'It was impressive,' my colleague recounted to me, 'a full kit inspection, in glorious Technicolor, right in front of me.' Grave loss of oriental face.

These weekly comings and goings, but without such embarrassing detail, were reported each week in our little plant newsletter, *Albayan*, produced in both Arabic and English and circulated widely not only to our workforce but throughout the island, to government, major companies and leading merchants. In the absence of fact, rumours are easy to start, particularly concerning our still poor safety record. The level of awareness began to change; the tactics I had employed as editor of the *Gulf Mirror* were serving me in good stead in the great wide world, a

The stamp collectors' cover produced by the author,
marking the first visit to Bahrain by Concorde

poacher turned gamekeeper. I had made the transition from
journalism to heavy industry almost as a matter of course. One
English wife came up to me at a reception and inquired about my
new role. 'You must miss the hurly-burly of newspapers terribly,'
she said well-meaningly. I could truthfully tell her that I never
even thought about it.

Though the plant was in the desert, we did have near-
neighbours, the little fishing villages of Askar and Jau, whose
inhabitants had originally settled in Bahrain from Qatar. They
lived a quiet existence on small incomes, periodically augmented
by the Ruler, who was always careful to make sure they were
reasonably content. The threat of a return whence they had come,
across the water, would be enough to pry loose the purse strings;
returning to their previous home with a tale of woe would reflect
badly on their adopted country's reputation for hospitality. But
these villagers were a big-hearted people and I was able to
establish a friendly relationship, helped by my aide Jassim Al-
Almeer as a go-between. Supplies of fresh water had become a
problem and we arranged a regular delivery service with a bowser
filled from our small desalination plant.

I became a regular guest at Askar for the traditional feast of a sheep marking the end of Ramadhan and the start of the Eid celebrations, seated on the floor and trying to keep up with my hosts as they ate at speed, rolling the highly-spiced rice into balls in the right hand and popping them into the mouth. Side dishes included the small *safi* fish caught in the nets we could see from the open doorway. Never before have I seen food disappear so quickly, as the women and children waited in the kitchen to take their turn – this was a masculine society. The head of Askar was well into his eighties, and the subject of much ribbing; he had married again, I was told, to a bride only in her early teens, and she was now pregnant. Another senior elder was blind. I was asked if there was a job for him at the smelter. 'Doing what?' Jassim asked. 'Perhaps a *natoor* (watchman),' came the deadpan reply.

In those early days we weren't always as careful about our housekeeping as we should have been. Waste oil from the host of tractors and vehicles at the plant was collected and then picked up by a contractor in his tanker. We gave little thought as to what happened to it thereafter, but it transpired he simply drove down to the beach and dumped it into the sea. The floating oil formed a slick as it drifted down the coast and began to clog the fish traps and nets of our village neighbours. Eventually they could ignore it no longer. An official meeting was sought with the smelter's management. They drove up in battered cars and pick-ups and the usual ritual unfolded. Introductions, routine pleasantries, solicitous inquiries into our health, all with a quiet dignity, until finally, the meeting almost at an end, the real reason for their visit was gently broached. We promised at once to do something about it. 'Action this day.' Our apologies were profuse, and the gathering broke up with relieved smiles. We all then adjourned to the main cafeteria, where I had taken the precaution of arranging a sumptuous lunch to smooth any ruffled feelings that might remain.

Our engineers began work on an oil trap, a device with six-foot-high cement walls into which waste liquid was poured. Any oil was separated and the remaining dirty water which sank to the bottom could be discharged harmlessly. Then the oil would be pumped out and disposed of periodically. The village delegation was invited back. Again, the ritual meeting, but this time with a formal procession to view the newly-finished oil trap, with Jassim providing the technical explanation as they peered into it, incongruous with white plastic safety helmets perched on top of their headdresses. Then again, a lavish meal, and quiet satisfaction on all sides. There was an unfortunate postscript, alas, but one which no one knew about and which I took care to keep to myself. When the oil trap was full, the contractor was summoned and it was pumped out into his tanker. Everyone knew of the pollution problem with the villages, but no one had thought to tell the contractor. He drove straight out of the plant, straight down to the beach, and dumped the contents into the water. Just like he'd always done.

One of the great strengths of the workforce was the British contingent, whose good humour often helped save the day when difficult situations threatened. They took to life in Bahrain with a zest, and in no time we had cricket teams, tennis tournaments, sailing, and soccer teams formed with the Bahrainis, who were and still are soccer mad, with an interest in England's top sides bordering on obsession. Our Brits had a ready wit and could be irrepressible. One foreman arrived late one day, and at lunchtime was asked what had delayed him. 'On the way to work, I knocked a young boy off his bike,' he confessed. There was consternation. 'What happened?' 'I solved it,' he explained nonchalantly. 'I gave him a dinar and told him to fuck off.' That throwaway phrase entered into company parlance. Whenever a problem arose, or if anyone was being awkward, it would come into use: 'Give him a dinar and tell him to fuck off . . . '

Rapid riposte was very much in evidence from the smelter's power station chief, John Little, ex-BP and sportsman extraordinary, who played cricket, golf, tennis and squash almost to a professional standard. His easygoing manner and laid-back approach belied a total professional. He was responsible for the smooth running of the 19 gas turbines that the smelter operated in harness, a feat never done anywhere else in the world at that time. One of his staff had recently recruited a maid from the Far East, from a country where morals were renowned for being lax. To the keen interest of the man's colleagues, it transpired that during his family's absence in England on holiday, the maid's duties had been extended. When this was brought to John's attention, quick as a flash he shot back: 'He's not paying her as well, I hope.'

Our Brits could also be on the receiving end. Gordon Bones and ex-Marine Harry Murt, two of our best maintenance men, were visiting London during one of their vacations, a city neither was used to. With their wives safely out of the way, they ended up in Soho and decided to visit a strip club. Fifteen later, minus a fairly large sum for admittance and for only a modest drink, they found themselves back on the pavement. Greatly angered, but knowing the club had several large heavies on duty, they spotted a police-man on the street corner. They went up to him. 'We've just been ripped off,' one of them protested. The bobby turned round, looked them up and down and displayed a very typical British *sang froid*. 'Fuck off,' he muttered out of the corner of his mouth. And they did.

Work at the smelter was hard, and in the heat of a Bahrain summer, wearing. Such conditions inevitably helped create a large demand for cold beer. The main hotels were too far away for regularly daily visits, and drinking at home a little boring. Aidan Westby, one of the engineering staff, came up with a novel idea. He would turn his home into a bar. The Engineers' Club was born, and proved an immediate hit. Every night until the small hours it would be thronged with Alba employees, Brits, Europeans and Bahrainis themselves, who could drink to their hearts' content. Aidan was married, but alas the union did not withstand the rigours of running a bar in his own home; it proved too much for his long-suffering wife who would come home from her job in Manama to face the hurly-burly of something resembling a cowboy saloon in the Wild West. Inevitably, they split, but the Engineers' Club went from strength to strength, eventually moving into its own premises in the nearby fertile coastal strip of Budaia.

But it was all unofficial. And one day I got a call from the government's Director of Labour, Khalifa Khalfan, a friend, who wanted to see me. He questioned me about the club, and told me he was considering closing it down. I pointed out that it had many Bahraini members, was properly run, there was never any trouble, and it also fulfilled a useful purpose. He agreed it could stay, and the club became official. I never told the organisers how close they had come to losing it.

Despite the sometimes arduous working conditions, life in Bahrain was good for the many staff and their families. But tragedies could happen. Two of the smelter's technical staff were called into the personnel office one day and told their wives had been in a bad car accident and were in hospital, in a serious condition. The women, both blonde, had been in a car which was hit by another driven by a member of the ruling family. The husbands reached the hospital to be told that one of the victims had already died, but neither could be identified because of the extent of their injuries. Neither wanted to view the survivor, terrified that it might not be his wife. Eventually one summoned up his nerve. He entered the hospital room and after some minutes, came out. 'I'm sorry,' he told his distraught colleague. 'It's not your wife, it's mine.' But his relief was brief; the next day she too died, and both men flew back to England with the bodies of their wives in coffins in the aircraft hold. Remarkably, both returned to work at the smelter, having made arrangements for relatives to care for their children. One was able to pick up his old life again, seemingly without problem. For the other, the memory of his lost wife was too traumatic. He had a breakdown and was repatriated to his family in England, where he stayed.

Periodic unrest was a feature of life in Bahrain, and trouble would flare in Manama over seemingly innocuous things. Alba was not immune from these upheavals, and complaints began to be made among our Bahrainis about some aspect of pay. Tension slowly grew, to the point when walk-outs began to happen, with intimidation of other staff, and the buses started to arrive at the plant empty when they should have been full, for the start of a shift. The atmosphere was like a pressure cooker, and somehow the plant was kept in production with a skeleton staff working massive amounts of overtime. After days of this mounting drama, it was decided that enough was enough. The dour chief of police, Jimmy Bell, a Carlisle man and former RAF bomber pilot, took the decision to send in the riot squad. They arrived on the back of lorries immediately, burly helmeted Baluchis carrying shields and the heavy cane lathis, eager for some real action after months of non-stop training for just such an eventuality. The mounting pressure vanished like a popped balloon as they set up camp outside the main gates, their gaily coloured blankets flapping outside the tent walls.

We paid for announcements on the local television, offering generous bonuses for those prepared to return to work during this unofficial strike, and slowly they began to come back, often, I learned later, at the insistence of wives who wanted the extra money, particularly when they heard of neighbours who were coining it in. The handful of troublemakers at the plant were rounded up, but not before a group, fleeing the advance of the lathi-swinging Baluchis, had headed straight for a fence of reinforced chainlink wire, smashed through it and vanished into the desert beyond. 'They went through the fence just like chips,' said an impressed British foreman. The excitement evaporated, life slowly returned to normal, and we went back to business as usual, but not before several hundred of our workforce, expatriates included, had made themselves quite a lot of extra cash, spent in the suq on hi-fis, televisions and cassette players.

Throughout all this I had kept the *Gulf Mirror*, and also the press in Britain and Europe, informed about what was happening, and the progress made. Alba came out of the episode with its reputation for fairness enhanced. And for me, it was time to move on. I had done what I had set out to do, turn Alba into a recognised brand-name as far as the industry was concerned, raised its profile in the technical and financial press, and played a part in making the plant accepted as part of the life of Bahrain.

A new adventure beckoned, this time in the heart of London, setting up a company for Arab interests with a promising young Bahraini businessman, Abdulnabi Al-Shoala, later to become a Cabinet minister, that would spread the word about Bahrain and the Gulf to a wider audience, to businesses seeking to invest, to companies looking to establish a foothold in the Middle East, and to travellers wanting a destination with a difference.

As we began preliminary work to lay the ground, I was surprised to receive a call from James Belgrave. He requested a meeting at his office. Puzzled, I drove down to see him. He came straight to the point. He was ending his association with the Mayfair public relations company and was about to set up his own operation to represent Bahraini interests. He thought I was just the man to join him. I was flabbergasted. Could this man, who had done so much to frustrate me, an albatross round my neck throughout my time on the *Gulf Mirror*, could he really be serious? He was. True to form, his grasp on reality was tenuous. This was a compliment I did not need and I politely turned him down, making no mention of my own intentions. Abdulnabi and I duly travelled to London to look for offices off Park Lane.

I told the Ruler of my plans. Even while I was at Alba we had kept in close contact. He was concerned for me, yet gave the enterprise his blessing. 'Don't leave us for ever,' he said. 'Some day you will come back.' With a heavy heart I took my leave of him, for the last time. As I emerged into the palace courtyard from his private office, I was again met by the heat of the day and brilliant sunshine that soon I would leave behind.

Since coming to Bahrain my world had been transformed. Life, I thought, could never be the same again. And it wasn't. Different, yes, but never the same. I had been fortunate to see traditional Bahrain at its best, an earlier, gentler way of life before the full force of modernisation had transformed it and its people for ever. The pace was slower then on an island that today has its own Formula One motor racing track and a population which has grown to a million people, including foreigners. It was a sad leave-taking. Ahead lay new challenges, but this particular odyssey was over. I had travelled to a far-off land, in Arabia, and now I was leaving. But a part of my heart would always remain. And in the years ahead, whenever I met an Arab, I would always say in Arabic, with pride: 'I am a Bahraini.'